AN ESSAY
by
RICK BASS

THE
NINEMILE
WOLVES

Library of Congress Cataloging-in-Publication Data
Bass, Rick, 1958–
   The Ninemile wolves / Rick Bass.
   p.   cm.
   Includes bibliographical references.
   ISBN 0-944439-47-0 (hard cover : acid free paper) : $22.95
   1. Wolves—Montana—Ecology.   2. Wildlife reintroduction—
Environmental aspects—Montana.   I. Title.
QL737.C22B37   1992
639.9'7974442—DC20   91-58687
                                                        CIP

Limited edition ISBN: 0-944439-48-9
Interior drawings copyright © 1992 by Russell Chatham.
Photographs on page 144 copyright © by Joe Fontaine, page 157 copyright
© by Mike Jimenez, page 138 copyright © by Layne Kennedy, page 159
copyright © by Rick McIntyre, page 162 copyright © by Tom Murphy, page
136 copyright © by John Murray, pages 150, 153, 155 copyright © by
Geoffrey Sutton, pages 140, 142 copyright © by Ralph Thisted, page 158
copyright © by Art Wolfe, pages 146, 148 copyright © by Ted Wood.

Portions of this book appeared in a different form in Outside and Icarus,
and acknowledgment is made to those magazines.

Clark City Press
Post Office Box 1358
Livingston, Montana   59047

FOR MY BROTHERS, FRANK AND B.J.;

OUR FATHER, CHARLIE;

AND OUR MOTHER,

MARY LUCY ROBSON BASS

Books by
Rick Bass

WILD TO THE HEART

THE DEER PASTURE

THE WATCH

OIL NOTES

WINTER: NOTES FROM MONTANA

THE NINEMILE WOLVES

ACKNOWLEDGMENTS

I owe many people thank yous for the gift of their professional
time. Renée Askins, head of the Wolf Fund, introduced me to
wolves—to the idea that they could come back to the West. I saw
my first wolves in Yaak, Montana, in the summer of 1988—two
huge silver wolves, with legs as long as stilts, right on the Canada–Montana border, over toward Idaho. The image remained
in my mind for eleven months, bright but ungerminated. Then
I met Askins in a wonderful *wolves ex machina*—I was walking
down a dusty road in the West, and she stopped and picked me
up and told me about wolves.

Ed Bangs, Steve Fritts, and Joe Fontaine of the U.S. Fish and
Wildlife Service in Helena, Montana, gave whatever I asked;
Mike Jimenez, also with the U.S. Fish and Wildlife Service, did
the same, and more.

John Murray, Peggy Shumaker and Carolyn Kremers, in
Alaska, were enthusiastic about keeping me updated with the
goings-on of wolves in that state; personnel from the Alaska Department of Fish and Game were also generous. Jay Gore and
Jeff Haas in Idaho, the famed veterinarian Dr. Doug Griffiths in
Libby, Montana, Warren Parker of the successful red-wolf project, and Dennis Parker, with his knowledge of Mexican wolves—
these people gave. Doug Peacock showed me his secret wolf spot
in Glacier; I still owe him mine in Yaak. Bob Ream and Mike

Fairchild answered all questions at all times of the day and night. All the biologists' *care* for wolves is extraordinary.

Reporter Sherry Devlin of the *Missoulian* introduced me to the story of the Marion wolves, and then the Ninemile wolves. She was dependable and exhaustive in her daily coverage of those stories as they unfolded. I owe editorial thank yous to Jamie and Steve Potenberg at Clark City Press and to Don Webster at *Outside* magazine; and pretty book thank yous to Stacy Feldmann, Anne Garner, and Russell Chatham at Clark City Press.

Thank you to the photographers Layne Kennedy, Tom Murphy, Rick McIntyre, Geoff Sutton, Ted Wood, and Art Wolfe. The biologist Mollie Matteson gave spirited and vigorous opinion on much of this book in her capacity as a fact checker, and the book is better and straighter because of her.

Books to which I am especially indebted are David Mech's *The Wolf*, Barry Lopez's *Of Wolves and Men*, David Brown's *The Wolf in the Southwest*, Peter Matthiessen's *Wildlife in America*, and Stanley Young's *The Last of the Loners*. Technical papers by Lee Anne Ayres, W. B. Ballard, Diane Boyd, Mike Fairchild, Steve Fritts, Paul Krausman, David Mech, Bill Paul, D. H. Pletscher, Kathryn Roney, Bob Ream and Ted Spraker were helpful, as was Bert Lindler's series in the May 1990 *Great Falls Tribune*.

Interesting additional information for and about wolves can be gotten from The Wolf Fund, P. O. Box 471, Moose, Wyoming 83012. The Montana Wilderness Association (P. O. Box 635, Helena, Montana 59624) deals with issues affecting wolves directly and indirectly, as does a curious and spirited organization, Moms Against Marlenee, chaired by Susan Donnelly (227 Trinkus Lane, Bigfork, Montana 59911). The Wildlife Damage Review evaluates government actions against predators and publishes a newsletter alerting the public about what can be done to stop abuses of various predator eradication programs. Information about the WDR can be gotten by writing them at Wildlife Damage Review, P. O. Box 2541, Tucson, Arizona 85702.

As generous as all these people (and many more) were with their knowledge of wolves, greatest and simplest thanks without question should go to the Thisted brothers—the two ranchers in the Ninemile who had the gentle temerity as well as the inquisitiveness to not panic when the wolves first appeared on their land. I think that, as with the old woman in the orchard (Irene Newman), the wolves sought these people.

What was lost, in this whole story—two steers, and two lambs? May we all never be judged by anything so harshly or held to as strict a life or unremitting of borders as the ones we try to place on and around wolves.

Rick Bass
January 1992

THE
NINEMILE
WOLVES

ONE

They say not to anthropomorphize—not to think of them as having feelings, not to think of them as being able to think—but late at night I like to imagine that they are killing: that another deer has gone down in a tangle of legs, tackled in deep snow; and that, once again, the wolves are feeding. That they have saved themselves, once again. That the deer or moose calf, or young dumb elk is still warm (steam rising from the belly as that part which contains the entrails is opened first), is now dead, or dying.

They eat everything, when they kill, even the snow that soaks up the blood.

This all goes on usually at night. They catch their prey from behind, often, but also by the nose, the face, the neck—whatever they can dart in and grab without being kicked. When the prey pauses, or buckles, it's over; the prey's hindquarters, or neck, might be torn out, and in that manner, the prey flounders. The wolves swarm it, then. They don't have thumbs. All they've got is teeth, long legs, and—I have to say this—great hearts.

I can say what I want to say. I gave up my science badge a long time ago. I've interviewed maybe a hundred people for or against wolves. The ones who are "for" wolves, they have an agenda: wilderness, and freedom for predators, for prey, for everything. The ones who are "against" wolves have an agenda: they've got vested financial interests. It's about money—more and more money—for them. They perceive the wolves to be an obstacle to frictionless cash flow.

The story's so rich. I can begin anywhere.

I can start with prey, which is what controls wolf numbers (not the other way around), or with history, which is rich in sin, cruelty, sensationalism (poisonings, maimings, torture). You can start with biology, or politics, or you can start with family, with loyalty, and even with the mystic-tinged edges of fate, which is where I choose to begin. It's all going to come together anyway. It has to. We're all following the wolf. To pretend anything else—to pretend that we are protecting the wolf, for instance, or *managing* him—is nonsense of the kind of immense proportions of which only our species is capable.

We're following the wolf. He's returning to Montana after sixty years.

The history of wolves in the West—of wolves in this country—is pretty well documented. Even by the turn of the century they were being diminished, and the wolves were all killed so quickly, and with such essentially religious zeal that we never had time to learn about them, and about their place on the land. And about our place on it. The wolves sure as hell didn't have time to learn about the government's wolf-, buffalo-, and Indian-killing program, and—well, I've got to say it—cows. Our culture has replaced buffalo with cattle, and wolves kill and eat cows, sometimes.

Peter Matthiessen writes in *Wildlife in America* that "with the slaughter of the bison and other hoofed animals in the late nineteenth century, the wolves . . . turned their attention to . . . livestock, which was already abundant on the grasslands." In the absence of bison, there was the bison's replacement: cattle. The wolves preyed upon these new intruders, without question, but ranchers and the government overreacted just a *tad*. Until very recently, the score stood at Cows, 99,200,000; Wolves, 0.

It took a lot of money to kill every last wolf out of the West. We behaved badly doing it: setting them on fire, feeding them ground-up glass, et cetera. Some people say it was the ranchers who kept the wolves out; others say the government. Other people say this country's lost its wildness, that it's no place for a wolf anymore, that already, wolves are like dinosaurs. There's room for sheep and cows, yes, and deer and elk and other plant eaters—but these woods are not the same woods they were sixty years ago. Even the shadows of trees in the forest are different, the wind's different.

There are a lot of people who believe that last part: that predators are out of date. And that Rocky Mountain gray wolves are the most old-fashioned, out-of-date predator of all. Sometimes I detect, even among wolves' most ardent well-wishers, a little chagrin that wolves succumbed so *easily*: that they wilted before the grazing juggernaut and federal predator-extinction programs of the 1920s. But with the government having been honed into fighting trim by practice on the "Indian problem," the wolves really had no chance. What's interesting (and wise) is that once the West's wolves were exterminated, they *stayed* exterminated. Canada's wolves did not repopulate the gaping wound of our wolf-free country.

Canada's always had the wolves, about 50,000 of them; so

many wolves that there's even been a "hunting" (read: *killing*—people don't eat wolves) season on them. Which may not be so bad, in places, because it probably helps keep those wolves wild. With the mild winters of the greenhouse eighties, ungulate populations have increased dramatically. Using Canada as a base, wolves, or rumors of wolves, have historically trickled across the border, making shy, hidden, and often ill-fated sorties into the U.S., hanging out in the deep timber of northwestern Montana, eating deer and trying to stay away from people. The prey that wolves chase is most often found in valley bottoms—along rivers, where ranches and villages are located. I like to think of the wolves hanging back in the woods, up in the mountains, *longing* for the river bottoms, but too wild, too smart, to descend. The deer down along the rivers, among the people, among the barking dogs, among the intricate road systems, are in a way protected from everything but overpopulation, disease and starvation.

The wolves watching those tempting Montana river bottoms, and longing, but then—wild—drifting back into Canada.

But the thing that defines a wolf more than anything—better than DNA, better than fur, teeth, green eyes, better than even the low, mournful howl—is the way it *travels*. The home range of wolves in the northern Rockies averages 200 to 300 square miles, and ranges of 500 square miles are not uncommon. Montana could not be avoided by Canadian wolves. There are too many deer, too many elk: too many for the few predators that still exist.

Glacier National Park, right on the Montana–Canada line, has sometimes harbored a pack, sometimes two, but that's all. In Glacier, the Magic and Wigwam and Camas packs averaged between fifteen and thirty animals in the 1970s and 1980s. The Wigwam pack held the most mystery—eight of their nine members simply disappeared, over the course of a few days in 1989. Poaching is suspected, but they could also have been "assassinated"—wolves will often fight to the death if another pack crosses their boundary. (Deer have learned to seek out these boundaries, the line between two packs' territories acting as a sort of demilitarized zone—a ridge separating two valleys, perhaps, or an uplift between two river forks.)

The Glacier wolves served as a hope, a *longing*, for the rest of Montana, and gave lovely possibility to the occasional rumors that leapt up around the area, in nearby valleys—the Tobacco and Yaak valleys to the west and Swan Valley to the south. But the wolves that left Glacier, if they were indeed the ones being spotted, never (to any scientist's knowledge) mated—never formed what the biologists call the "pair bond" of an alpha male and alpha female—and it was thought that the sightings were unusually large coyotes. There's not as much similarity between the two as you'd think: coyotes often have a lot of red in their coats, and their muzzles are sharper, reminding me of screwdrivers, and their ears are larger and more pointy-looking. Coyotes are 25 percent to 50 percent smaller than long-legged wolves, and wolves have "fur around their face," and a ruffed coat, like a cape, up across their shoulders; coyotes' necks look bare by comparison.

Rumors of wolves outside of Glacier kept drifting in, increasing steadily through the 1980s, which fanned the hopes of those people desiring wolves. A poll taken in 1990 showed that two-thirds of Montanans believed wolves should be allowed to return to the state, while one-third thought wolves should be locked out. In the summer of 1988, in my valley, a mile south of Canada, I saw two big gray wolves—a mated pair, I hoped—lope through the woods, running north, headed to the border; later that winter, friends told me they'd seen a big black wolf and a gray wolf on the other side of their frozen lake, on several mornings, which indicated there might possibly, hopefully, be a pack. They're filtering south, even as you're reading this—moving through the trees, mostly, and eating a deer about every third day; they're coming down out of Canada, and the wild ones are trying to stay out of the populated river bottoms. The less wild ones—well, sometimes people see those.

It's been theorized that in addition to Montana's high deer population, hunting pressure in Canada may be helping send wolves back south, all along the U.S.–Canadian border—into the Cascades, the Olympics, northern Idaho and northwestern Montana, even along Montana's Front Range—but the main reason seems to be game overabundance, a dangerous excess, the simple response of predator-and-prey cycles. Like the tides and the pull of the moon, it's not a thing that we've been able to mess up, yet. It still works, or tries to. The recent warm winters in Montana have led deer and elk populations to all-time highs. There haven't been any dramatic disease die-offs in recent memory, no massive winter kills, no outbreaks of starvation and land-gone-ragged. The deer populations keep climbing as if *desiring* that outcome, though, and each summer you see more and more fawns; each fall you see more and more deer. The deer have the run of the woods, though mountain lion populations are increasing rapidly to join in on the feast. You've got to drive slowly at night. It's hard to find anyone living in the country who hasn't struck a deer at least once, late at night, no matter how carefully he drives. Usually if you hit a deer, you stop and put it in the back of your truck and drive on home and clean it and eat it (illegal, of course, but not immoral)—but sometimes the out-of-town people will keep going after striking a deer, leaving the deer dead on the side of the road or even *in* the road, and in the morning, if you live nearby, you'll hear the ravens, and then later in the afternoon, the little slinky-dog coyotes barking at one another, and by that night, everything's gone: meat, bones, hooves, even the hide.

I should point out that that's the scientists' belief—that Montana's huge deer populations are bringing the wolves back. There is another thought that occurs to me, though I'm sure the scientists would have nothing to do with this idea. I've been reading all the old case histories of wolves in this country and following the new histories, and the species doesn't seem to have changed in a hundred years, a hundred generations. The intricacy of their pack structure—the hierarchy of dominance and submission— is well documented, as is their territoriality, their fierce protection of borders, and their love of travel, of exploring those borders.

But these new wolves—I get the sense that they're a little different. Wiser, of course—even if only bearing wise blood but not knowing it. They seem to be a little *edgier*—pushing for those edges. All wolves travel like crazy, but these new wolves seem a little restless even for their species. They're trying to trickle down, like roots spreading fingers into weathered rock. And this time we'll be able to find out if human nature, and our politics, have changed—metamorphosed, perhaps, into something more advanced—or if at the base our politics are still those of Indian killers.

The wolves intend to find out, too.

Everything travels fast for a wolf. They went from huge buffalo-supported packs of twenty and thirty animals to near-extinction with great speed, and it is in their blood to recover with great speed, given the right conditions. Sixty years is only a blink, and it is a predator's genetic duty to endure hard times— very hard times—along with the sweet times.

The old wolves were natives, residents. These new wolves are foreigners, pioneers: explorers. It could be argued that wolves are never more wolflike than when they're exploring, trying to claim, or reclaim, new territory, rather than holding on and defending old borders. It could be argued that our perverse resistance to wolves helps them *remain* wolves, that they need that great arm's distance to remain always outside of other communities, except perhaps for the community of ravens.

Is the base of our history unchanging, like some *batholith* of sin—are we irretrievable killers?—or can we exist with wolves, this time? I believe we are being given another chance, an opportunity to demonstrate our ability to change. This time, we have a chance to let a swaying balance be struck: not just for wolves, but for humans, too. If I could say any one thing to politicians, and to people with guns and poison (and sheep and cows), it would be this: that to have the balance the majority of people claim to long for, it must be struck by the wolves as much as by the people. The wolves must have some say in defining it, or it will not be valid. And since they do not speak our language, it might be rough for a while: for three years, or five years, or maybe even ten.

I'd always thought of the "typical" wolf as being a smoke-gray color, but the wolves from Glacier are solid black half the time. It took me a while to get used to this—the black ones seemed, in my mind, more like dogs—but now I prefer seeing the black ones; the shining black coat sets off their green eyes in a way that seems to give the eyes more internal fire than they already have.

Old-timers around the town of Libby tell how there used to be a lot of wolves in the Yaak Valley at the turn of the century, and how so many of them were black. I like a black wolf, though this is a long story, and there's not going to be time for what I do or don't like.

Wolf packs in northwestern Montana average between six and ten animals. These numbers are a function of both the social characteristics of the individuals within the pack and of game size and availability. It doesn't take many wolves to hunt the ubiquitous white-tailed deer. There's lots of game, and not many established wolf territories yet; a lot of free country just for the taking, room for "dispersers"—ambitious, aggressive, or outcast lone wolves—to expand into. It's an eerie form of recapitulation, not unlike, perhaps, our own species' westward expansion two hundred years ago. One healthy wolf can bring down one white-tail by itself. If a wolf in northwestern Montana isn't an alpha (breeding) wolf but desires to be, there's nothing to prevent him or her from taking off across the next ridge and over into the next valley, which, for now, is probably not wolf-occupied—containing instead only deer, elk and moose, and probably people, and maybe cattle.

In parts of Alaska and Minnesota, on the other hand, other packs' territories are already "taken," and the primary prey species is often moose. This creates more pressure to stay in a pack, even if it means being a beta or more subordinate pack member. It takes at least three or four wolves, absolute minimum, to bring down a moose, and the packs do better with around a dozen.

The one exception to this Montana average of six to ten animals—and that's the lovely thing about wolves, you can never count on them to be counted on—was the giant pack that built up in Glacier, the Camas pack. It numbered, briefly, *twenty* members, and has since split into two packs, north and south, which range along the Flathead River. Because they're all family it's thought that—unlike other packs—the Camas wolves won't fight to the death if they stray into each other's territory. Mollie Matteson, a biologist in Montana, reports that members of the north and south packs even visited each other's dens in the summer of 1990, with "considerable going back and forth." (The alpha female of the north pack is the mother of the breeding female in the south pack.)

So Glacier's doing okay for wolves, for now. Soon enough—too soon—this story is going to have to lead away from wolf sociology and enter the dense woods of human sociology, and once that forest is entered, it may be a long time before the wolves in question emerge. I want to hold off from entering that place for as long as I can. Once the wolves in question get into that tangle of bureaucracy and human pinball, biological lies and manipulations, there's no telling where the wolves will emerge finally—or if they'll simply vanish—but already, in this story, they're moving inexorably toward that dark grove.

Usually the image one gets of wolves is of a deer running through the forest, with the wolves close behind. But in this forest, the image I get is of the wolf pack running through the trees, hurdling logs, with people chasing them, people running close behind. Not just ranchers and wolf-lovers are following them, but men and women in suits—politicians, and worse—and scientists, too, with all sorts of drugs and needles and electrical equipment. Some of the wolves will be captured and will succumb or be tamed, but others will break off from the pack that's being pursued, will escape, and continue weaving through the woods. As long as there are a lot of deer, these dispersers have a chance—a good chance.

Despite their deer-catching skills and wild, leave-away hearts, the odds for survival are stacked a little higher against disperser wolves. Wolf biologist Diane Boyd has documented wolves leaving the Glacier area and traveling as far as 500 miles. David Mech begins one of the chapters in his book, *The Wolf*, with an old Russian proverb that says, "The wolf is kept fed by his feet"—but traveling, and movement, seems to feed the wolf's soul, as well; it's nothing for them to cover twenty miles overnight on a hunt. The farthest recorded twenty-four-hour distance was traveled by a wolf in Scandinavia that went 125 miles in a day and a night, under pressure from dogs and hunters.

The farthest overall dispersal is 1500 kilometers (over 829 miles) by a wolf in Canada, an act which, if undertaken by any of the Glacier wolves, would put them clearly into the prey-infested woods of Yellowstone. Three more hops and a skip, as in the movement of a knight on a chess board, would take them back into southern Colorado, one of the country's areas richest in wolf lore. Yellowstone is supposedly another story from what this book's about—the biologists for the U.S. Fish & Wildlife Service (USF&WS) say, "Don't get this mixed up with Yellowstone"—but one thing I've learned in reading and asking about wolves in Montana over the last three years is that *nothing*'s a different story. It's all being woven together, more than a computer can hold, and certainly more than someone's mind—scientist or not—can assimilate.

What this story is about, this part of the weave, is the young Ninemile pack whose mother wandered all the way down into the country west of Missoula, into the mountains south and west of giant Flathead Lake, within easy striking distance of Idaho—within sight of Idaho, from the highest peaks. These pups raised themselves—were orphaned by fate while they still had their baby teeth—and in a brave move ripe with political festerings, were kept alive by USF&WS biologists whose job as mandated by federal law is "to preserve and protect endangered species," of which these six pups most certainly were: the Rocky Mountain gray wolf, *Canis lupus irremotus*. The Latin name, as *Missoulian* reporter Sherry Devlin has pointed out, translates roughly, wonderfully, into meaning "The Wolf Who Is Always Showing Up."

TWO

Where the story started for our species—where humans picked up on the scent and fell into the chase—was in Pleasant Valley, a long, narrow valley in northwestern Montana lying roughly midway between Glacier National Park and the town of Libby. Northwestern Montana's not great cattle country—it's too cold, too snowy, and there's not much grass (mostly timber, or steep rocks, or ragged moonscape clear-cuts)—but near the tiny village of Marion, in April of 1989, a two-year-old male wolf (probably not a Glacier wolf) tried to get in a sheep pen one night. The line of intersection between wolf and man in Montana had been crossed after roughly sixty years of silence,* and from this point there wouldn't be, and probably won't be, any turning back: no more silence.

Certain wolves will prey on cattle, and to a greater extent,

---

*There was one brief and fatal (for cows) flurry of cow-wolf interaction on the Blackfeet Reservation, east of the Continental Divide, in 1987.

upon hapless, irresistible sheep; anyone who tells you a wolf won't kill a cow or sheep is lying or misinformed. But there is an almost finite number of variables. Wild, healthy wolves tend to stay away from livestock. A wolf that has never been "taught" by its elders to hunt or eat livestock probably never will.

One of the trouble times for wolves as well as coyotes with regard to livestock depredation is in April, when the pups have just been born and the whole pack is hanging around the den for a few months, still unable to travel. Deer and elk in the area tend to get understandably spooked by a three-month wolf pack *encampment*. The wolves' nutritional demands are greater then, with extra hunting required to take care of the pups and, I propose (which I can do, being a writer and not a biologist), it's possible that the rest of the pack gets plain restless during the denning period. Typically (though not always) only the alpha male and female will have bred, and from April to July of each year the rest of the pack just stays near the den, waiting. The cattle call may beckon to restless wolves in the spring.

In July, the pack starts to move the pups a little farther from the den to "rendezvous" sites—usually places where some animal has been killed—and the pups begin to learn what the game's about by eating these on-site kills, and by chasing mice and grasshoppers. By late August or September, the pups, which grow quickly, are ready to start traveling, ready to start watching "real" hunts.

The wolf that had been—or rather, had allegedly been—trying to get in the Marion area sheep pen was shot and killed by the rancher; the rancher said he thought it was a dog or coyote, but when he realized it could be a wolf, he called authorities. The incident was investigated by USF&WS agents, and the rancher wasn't prosecuted. It turned out ranchers and other residents had been hearing wolves for some time prior to the shooting, but hadn't reported them for the usual reason: fear that all kinds of federal restraints might be placed upon the valley. Some kind of quarantine, perhaps, is how I picture the ranchers imagining it— a giant plastic bubble being placed over the valley, with a blood mist being sprayed by helicopter every six hours to further incite the wolves, and ranchers being handcuffed to their beds each night as they listen to the bleats and bawls of their sheep and cattle . . .

The reality is that wolves preying on livestock on private lands are "removed" immediately, and there is little doubt that this is anything but beneficial to both wolf and rancher, though there are numerous cases where wolves have stopped killing cattle after two or three depredations. The line has been crossed—humans have contacted wolves again, and wolves have contacted humans—and it's important for the wolves and the humans that we try to avoid the bitter polarization that characterizes other environmental battles. Readers should note at this point in the story that there hadn't been any livestock depredation—just howling—although a wolf (maybe the two-year-old male, but maybe another, older male) had been seen among livestock on several occasions. Because there's a $100,000 fine and a one-year jail term for killing a wolf, ranchers were concerned, seeing this wolf frolic with their livestock, but were hesitant to try to remove it themselves.

In late July, four months after the two-year-old was killed in a sheep pen, a wolf rendezvous site (and possible den) was discovered only three miles from the sheep corral. USF&WS personnel asked the rancher to let them leave the wolves on his ranch until late August—to let the pups mature. Wolf packs are wired so intricately, with such complexity, that there's not a single record of a pack being busted up by humans and then reassembling itself. The rancher agreed to let the pups stay on his land through the month. He frequently observed the wolves hunting small mammals among his cattle.

After August the pack's integrity would be destroyed if trapped and relocated, but the individuals should survive. Things were just too tense: too many cattle, too many sheep, too close to the wolves. The USF&WS had data from Minnesota that showed pups had high survival chances after August even if separated from their pack, and if the pups weighed over thirty-five pounds. These numbers, while ultimately not safe enough for the pups in the Marion case, may prove important to the rest of wolf history in the United States, and should be remembered, and perhaps increased slightly.

On August 21st, 1989, fortune's winds shifted. A domestic dog was attacked (allegedly) by two wolves—a large gray wolf and a smaller black one. Wild wolves *hate* dogs in their territory, viewing them as competitors, and kill and eat them with gusto. On that same day a rancher found five dead calves and one severely wounded calf.

On the 22nd of August, a USF&WS biologist, and an Animal Damage Control* specialist and a Montana Department of Fish, Wildlife & Parks (MDFWP) conservation officer checked out the remains. The battles had occurred in a pasture that had been holding exclusively sick and weakened calves. The data gathered by the federal officials and a veterinarian, wrote Ed Bangs, a federal wolf biologist down from Alaska, "suggested wolves were not responsible for injuries to the surviving calf but that the at-

*A federally and state-funded predator eradication program with an annual budget of $45,000,000.

tack came from a smaller 'inefficient' canine predator." There were, and still are, a lot of coyotes in the Marion area, and coyotes generally kill by choking the victim, rather than pulling the prey down from behind—grabbing the flanks with their teeth—which is more typical of wolves than coyotes.

Regardless of the lack of evidence against wolves—despite, in fact, evidence which pointed to coyotes—the USF&WS decided that day to proceed with their relocation; had already decided before the incident, in fact, to go ahead with it the very next day.

"One day," Ed Bangs lamented, stroking the black handlebar moustache that gives him the look of a circus lion tamer. "Just one more day, and we would have had them out of there."

Wolf recovery in Montana was in its most embryonic stages. This was the first known pack to have a den outside of the park* in over sixty years, the first *expansion*, and whether it was coyotes or wolves that had killed the livestock was irrelevant: The public perception was that wolves were in there doing the killing, and such a cow-killing catastrophe the first time wolves were seen out of the park could have meant the end of the wolf recovery program before it had really begun. I want to believe the wolves were pure—that it was coyotes who deviled those sick cows, and then the young wolves and alpha female moved in and scavenged afterward—but word was out, *belief* was out, and the situation wasn't going to disappear.

It took three days before traps (leg-hold, spring-action) could be set, due to rain. There are basically only two ways to catch wolves alive—by leg-hold traps, or by tranquilizing (darting)—and northwest Montana's timbered so heavily that the helicopter

*A den was found on the Blackfeet Reservation, east of Glacier, in 1987, which was believed to have been used that year.

chases so effective for getting close to wolves to tranquilize them are frequently impossible.

A third method of capture is sometimes available and should be mentioned, though it bears a certain repellence to the spirit: Trapped wolves may be fitted with radio collars which, in addition to transmitting the wolves' location, contain injectors which, so goes the theory, can be remote-controlled to fire tranquilizers into the wolf's neck, dropping the wolf long-distance, on command—a notion eerily similar to those high-pitched dog whistles advertised in boys' magazines, or worse yet, a leash.

The traps were set August 25th. Three wolves had been observed near the rendezvous site: a black female and two pups. Two of the pups (both female "young-of-the-year," born in April) were captured immediately. They weighed forty and forty-one pounds. It was still raining. The mother could not be caught, nor could any additional wolves. One of the greatest things about wolf packs is that you can never be entirely sure how many are in a pack. The social hierarchy of alpha male and alpha female, of baby-sitting aunts and occasionally uncles, and of outcasts living sometimes just out of sight of the pack, is always tense, ripe for change, and at least partially obscured to everyone but the wolves themselves. By the fall, even the pups, at sixty to eighty pounds, are hard to distinguish from the adults, who may weigh only seventy to one hundred pounds.

The pups were put in a veterinary clinic in Kalispell, then brought back out to the rendezvous site and placed in individual kennels in the hopes that the adult female would remain close to her pups' cages. Every three to four days thereafter, the pups were taken back into the clinic for examination. The state agency— the MDFWP—provided road-killed deer to keep the pups fed.

On August 28th, parts of a full-grown cow—hind leg, front

leg, ribs, vertebrae—were found at the wolves' rendezvous site, as were fresh wolf scats containing red and black cow hair. It's possible that the coyotes did the killing and then the larger remaining wolf, or wolves, might have run the coyotes off the kill. But in the climate of panic it didn't look good for the wolves, and in Minnesota such evidence would have been classified as "confirmed wolf depredation."

Two more days passed. USF&WS stayed in close contact with local ranchers and held a meeting in which, according to Ed Bangs, "only a couple of individuals seemed very upset about the presence of wolves." The ranchers' main concern, Bangs says, was what would happen back up in the woods, where the ranchers couldn't see what was going on—the eternal, lovely metaphor of the wolf's existence: his dark shape, just beyond the edge of the dark woods.

Another cow, a 300-pound calf, was killed in the same "sick" pasture. This made six known calf depredations. Coyotes were seen running from the carcass. Wounds—hemorrhaging in the throat—suggested coyotes. Coyote tracks and scats were all around the area. Bangs wrote, "Service personnel elicited howling from two large groups of coyotes near the pasture on several nights."

The next day, the calf that was still living but severely wounded was killed by the rancher and skinned and examined. Bite wounds indicated coyotes or, possibly, very young wolves, because the skin was never entirely punctured, only scraped, as if the predator had strangled the calf. In some places teeth had broken through the hide but in other places had only scraped the skin. One set of bites measured two and one-sixteenth inches wide, implying a wolf, but the bite marks could have come from two separate snaps.

Labor Day passed. Several coyotes were trapped, but no additional wolves. The two wolf pups continued to be shuttled back and forth from vet clinic to rendezvous site, to be used as a lure.

On September 7th, a new wolf showed up in one of the USF&WS traps: an old gray male with extreme tooth wear, including his canines. His teeth were more worn than any wolf the biologists had ever seen. His front left foot was injured by the trap. His front canine teeth measured two and one-sixteenth inches across.

It was time to get on with the show, to walk away from the issue or finish it. On September 8th, an Animal Damage Control (ADC) specialist shot the black female from a helicopter with an immobilizing drug, Telazol. It was a "great shot" from the helicopter, according to Ed Bangs, and she went down in only four minutes.

While under this drug, Telazol, the wolf is open-eyed, in a phase that the drug's manufacturer, the A. H. Robins Company, calls "cataleptoid anaesthesia." Do the cataleptoid wolves' open eyes relay to the mind what's going on, as they're handled by humans? No one can say for sure. The drug's pamphlet states that "the anaesthetic state produced does not fit into the conventional classification of states of anaesthesia, but instead . . . produces a state . . . which has been termed 'dissociative' anaesthesia in that it appears to selectively interrupt association pathways to the brain . . . cranial nerve reflexes remain active."

I hope that certain "associative pathways" do remain open, such as the pathways that take fear in and out of the brain. On the one hand, the terror for such a wild animal—being handled, and unable to flee—is probably unbearable; on the other hand— or so we might anthropomorphize—it could make the animal so wild and wary that its future survival ability might be heightened to new levels.

Telazol appears to be safe—certainly a quantum leap from the mind-altering tranquilizers used on Yellowstone grizzlies in the sixties and seventies. Telazol has resulted in less than 1 percent mortality and has been used successfully on polar bears, grizzlies, and wolverines. The breakthrough for Telazol lies in the combining of two components: tiletamine hydrochloride (which when used alone can produce convulsive seizures) and zolazepam hydrochloride (which when used alone can cause belligerence). But W. B. Ballard of the Alaska Department of Fish and Game, who has darted fifty-one wolves with Telazol, writes that "the undesirable characteristics of each drug are eliminated when the drugs are combined."

Thirteen of Ballard's fifty-one darted wolves were females, and six of the females were pregnant at the time but went on to give birth to litters with "no apparent side effects," though the Robins Company says that Telazol does cross the placental barrier and causes decreased respiration in the fetus.

There are minor side effects for the animals being darted: excessive salivation, retching, and eye desiccation from a lack of blinking while in the cataleptic state. A towel and bland ophthalmic ointment should be placed over the wolves' eyes. And trappers using Telazol must work quickly—the drug wears hard on the wolves' kidneys, and therefore should not be over-administered. Nonetheless, it appears to be safe; only one dog out of 1,072 tested in a lab died from the drug itself, though a few "geriatric" dogs had heart failure.

It takes between five and twelve minutes for a darted animal to go down. Behavioral characteristics of a darted wolf involve an initial "high stepping," writes Ballard, "followed by disoriented gait, loss of use of hind legs, licking lips, loss of use of forelegs, loss of head and neck movement . . . " Darted wolves remain cataleptic for an average of seventy minutes, though recovery time for Ballard's wolves ranged between half an hour to five hours.

Back in Marion, while the mother was being chased and darted, another young-of-the-year wolf pup was discovered still with her. Several attempts were made to drive the young wolf from the six-foot hay where it was hiding, but ADC officials couldn't flush it, and couldn't dart it in that deep grass. Later that evening Ed Bangs was driving his truck when he saw the third pup out in the field again, in the open and "not real nervous." Bangs drove out in the field, steering with one hand and firing the dart gun with the other, but he missed when the wolf started zigging.

"The wolf got into cover and looked back and then just walked off," Bangs said. That wolf would get wilder, of course—wild enough to survive, and remain untrapped, and to hook up with another wolf that winter—though in the spring it would be shot from an ADC helicopter when livestock depredation resumed in the Marion area, and efforts to trap it failed once again. "At least another wolf hooked up with it that winter," Bangs wrote.

It had been over two weeks since the roundup started. People were coming by the vet clinic to "visit the wolves." The fear was that the two pups were becoming "habituated to humans and objects representing civilization," wrote Bangs. USF&WS had picked out a relocation spot, the Great Bear Wilderness, on the other side of Glacier National Park. The Great Bear seemed to offer the wolves' best chance of survival because it was rich in game, had few to no livestock, and it was hoped its ruggedness would prevent the wolves' return to the Marion area. The area in the Great Bear where the feds wanted to release the wolves was not occupied by another wolf pack and hence there wouldn't be a bloodbath for "turf."

About this time—September—rumors (later confirmed) began to drift in that the Wyoming Farm Bureau was contemplating legal action to prevent the release. The USF&WS received information about a possible court injunction. Steve Fritts, head of the USF&WS Northern Rockies wolf recovery program, said later that the feds could have fought it in court while the wolves stayed in captivity, or the feds could have run from the Farm Bureau's suit—could have done what was necessary to get the wolves back on the ground as quickly as possible. They chose the latter.

September 13th was picked as the date to release the black female, her two young, and the old gray smooth-toothed male, whether or not the other pup had been caught. The pups were losing weight in captivity—one pound each, during a time when they should have been gaining. The male weighed ninety-seven pounds, the female seventy-eight pounds. They were fitted with radio collars. A makeshift pen would be constructed to hold the wolves for a while at the release site, to let them get used to the sounds and scents of the area—what's called a "soft" release, which has worked extremely well for red wolf relocations in the South. The pups would be given less tranquilizer than the adults, so that they would become alert before the adults did. Everyone knew the adults would run the second they woke up. The pups would have to be ready.

After the wolves were prepared for release, a news conference was held.

At noon that day, the state of Montana stepped in. Governor Stan Stephens (the first Republican governor in umpteen billion years), and his appointed director of the MDFWP, K. L. Cool, requested a briefing. After the briefing, Stephens, that wily biologist/governor, informed the feds that he wanted the wolves released in Glacier National Park, twenty miles from the federal biologists' original site. The feds cancelled their plans.

When the wolves woke up from their drugs, they were still in captivity. Logistics had to be planned anew for the state-mandated release site. It's curious how the state assumed control of the federal release of an endangered species onto federal lands, but they did. They continue to petition the courts to give them jurisdiction.

To stay out of court, the feds went along with Governor Stephens' politico-biology. Never mind that there were already wolf packs living in Glacier; it was about human hunters, about economics, and fears.

The next day, September 14th, 1989, the four wolves were sedated once again. Glacier has a small but dense population of grizzly bears, so food couldn't be left out for the wolf family, and the terrain was too rough for a temporary holding pen to be constructed.

When the wolves woke up from the drugs, they hit the ground running. The adults fled south, leaving the young wolves behind, and the young alpha female subsequently left the old male behind. USF&WS wolf biologist Mike Jimenez would say later that "all she was trying to do was get back to Marion," back to a place where she knew how to hunt, knew the terrain, knew her den— knew all the things it took to keep her species alive. Even if it meant sacrificing this year's litter.

The pups, as had been expected, didn't move far from the release site—three to five miles—though in the spot where the state ordered them dumped, three to five miles carried them into the rockiest, most game-scarce country available. The pups' limited range is a thing to consider, to hope for, in future relocations. They're too young to have developed that fierce, almost frantic sense of place, of home, that the adults have, and so in staying close to a well-chosen relocation spot, they might have a stab at survival.

But these pups were too young and traumatized.

On September 26th the first mortality signal came from one of the pups' radio collars. The pup had starved. Under ideal conditions, wolves are taught everything by their parents and by the pack and are brought along slowly, as is the way of most mammals. All manners of social skills are learned, the last and most important of which is hunting: of communicating their intent among one another and then working together to bring down not necessarily the largest available prey, but instead whatever it is they went out looking for that day.

David Mech writes in *The Wolf*, "One day I watched a long line of wolves heading along the frozen shoreline of Isle Royale, in Lake Superior. Suddenly they stopped and faced upwind toward a large moose. After a few seconds, the wolves assembled closely, wagged their tails, and touched noses. Then they started upwind single file toward the moose."

Biologists speak with complete conviction of wolves having "search images," and I visualize a seek-and-destroy mind-set reminiscent of submarine pilots, of computer grid coordinates flashing before the wolves' minds' eyes as they cast and weave through the woods, having somehow decided that day to go for a moose rather than a deer or elk, bypassing young deer huddled beneath fir trees, running right *over* the backs of snowshoe hares—focused only on that one certain missing image.

Of the three main ungulate prey species, the moose is the largest and hence most difficult and dramatic of takedowns for the pack: it requires both speed and sophistication. In many parts of Alaska, Canada and Minnesota, moose are the primary prey species—a fact reflected in those packs' larger sizes. Mike Jimenez, the USF&WS biologist I spent time with in Montana, understands how easily people will take a perception of the wolf and then twist it, fashion a handle for it, and carry it around to *use* it, incorrectly. Jimenez reminded me to remind people that moose are not the primary prey species in Montana, where packs rely instead on plentiful deer and elk.

"People get kind of funny," Jimenez says, "when you start talking about them killing moose."

These Marion young-of-the-year, these puppies, were not up for killing moose, or even elk or deer. USF&WS biologists discussed feeding the remaining collared pup by air-dropping carcasses to her. Things were far, far out of hand for wildlife purists—they had gotten out of hand for the purists beginning with the first trap setting, the first helicopter flight, not to mention the first radio collar (dogs wear collars!) and some Western ranchers had to be feeling a little left out, a little jealous. Why all this technological pampering for killers? Why can't *we* be the only killers, the only meat-eaters? At the other spectral end, there was a passionate group of people who believed that wild wolves were gold and that every stop should be pulled out, that every available means of life support should be used. Beyond that, there were people who believed that even the *idea* of wolves was gold, and that maybe hybrids were an answer—threatening to release their part dog, part wolf pets into the dark woods—animals that howled like wolves, and looked like wolves, to some degree. Blockier muzzles, and sometimes a slight curl to their tails; different DNA, and slightly more—shall we say—aggressive? *Psychotic?*

This was only one thin layer of the network, the political tangle, in which the USF&WS was trying to operate, as if in a net of ropes. Below lay the national concerns of Yellowstone, and all the associated political posturings and trumpetings—would these wolves move into Yellowstone? Montana Senator Conrad Burns has predicted that if wolves get back to Yellowstone "there'll be a dead child within a year." Montana's other progressive Congressman, Ron Marlenee, has said that wolves are "like cockroaches in your attic."

Below the Yellowstone tangle lay the strong net of state politics—of game and fish politics—which is to say, the politics of deer and elk availability to lard-ass hunters with no concept of simple biology but a healthy fear that wolves might compete with their high-powered scopes and 2900-feet-per-second bullets. The state game and fish department's principle in this matter seems to be slanted to the nineteenth-century American philosophy that, despite history's and nature's evidence to the contrary, more is better, a lot more is even better, and excess is best.

Somewhere below all these layers, there was one uncatchable "mystery" pup, back in Marion; one dead pup; and one skinny living one. There was one old gray tooth-worn male wandering around—his collar signals showed that he'd staked out a cattle ranch near Glacier—and one lope-away black female with a heart like a furnace, who was traveling, *Missoulian* reporter Sherry Devlin wrote, "incessantly."

The old gray male kept hanging around his new adopted ranch's cattle. A bandage had been placed on his injured foot, and when he walked it trapped the blood and acted as a tourniquet; perhaps with his worn teeth he couldn't chew the bandage off. (Six of one, half a dozen of the other; the biologists chose to bandage the wound to try and prevent it from becoming dirty and then infected . . .) The foot had developed gangrene—it would soon rot off the bone—and often he was observed just lying beneath a tree, watching the cattle. He was emaciated and wobbly when he walked. He was put out of his misery—shot—and weighed seventy-eight pounds when they took him in, a twenty-pound weight loss.

This isn't all the blind foul-up it appears to be. It's just the way wolves and humans are, together. It's like falling through a network of ropes, as if in a circus high-wire act—a slow tumble, bouncing from rope to rope, as if weaving, *vertically*, from top to bottom, with a lot of things being lost along the way: some wolves, some cows, some innocence . . .

Back when they'd first captured the old gray male, the USF&WS had considered *not* releasing him because, Ed Bangs wrote, "his advanced age seemed to indicate a relatively short period of survival in the wild." However, "The decision to release him reasoned that any period of survival in the wild would be preferable to spending the rest of his life in captivity. There were also expectations that he might provide food for the young-of-the-year wolves or possibly a mate for the adult female in the upcoming breeding season."

I'm encouraged when I read these words from a federal official, a G-man. They're well thought-out, specific considerations for the survival of the species, and for the survival of individuals. They just didn't work, this time; wrong guess. The gray male's foot was worse than it looked, and got infected, despite the vet's doctoring it. It's easy to knee-jerk react negatively to all feds, all agencies, but when I look at Bangs's statement, "It was reasoned that any period of survival in the wild would be preferable to spending the rest of his life in captivity," I see more than a glimmer of wild, anthropomorphic *yearning* beating in that sentence, glimmering like gold from a stream in the bright sunlight: hope.

The day after the old male was shot, the second pup died. It too starved up in the rock and ice country of Glacier National Park, just a few miles from the release site.

The remaining pup—the wild one still left at Marion—had disappeared. After nine days of looking for tracks and sign, and howling and listening, and checking the dozen traps they'd laid for it, no recent wolf activity could be detected.

The entire pack had been trapped in the political maze. Only the alpha female came out at the bottom, and she was heading south, along the far shores of Flathead Lake, passing right through the little town of Bigfork, where dogs roam the streets in large numbers, though they all escaped with their lives that night. Her radio signals showed that she passed right next to the little hydro dam powerhouse in the downtown area. Flathead Lake—the largest freshwater lake in the West—barred her return to Marion.

There were touching reports of people seeing her here and there. She had to be lonely. Wolves are the most social mammals in this part of the world, except (maybe) for humans. One old woman in Rattlesnake Canyon just outside of Missoula, Irene Newman, said she spotted a wolf in her backyard orchard, just resting in the shade. Newman heard her five dogs barking and looked out her window and saw a wolf "sauntering up the draw behind the house."

Newman went outside and called to the wolf. "I see you," she told the wolf, and the wolf stopped, looked at Newman, and then stepped back behind an apple tree.

"You're not hiding, I can see you," Newman said, and the wolf peeked around the tree and looked up at her—just stood there, looking at her.

At the time, Dale Harms of the USF&WS said that the black female's radio-collar signals showed she'd gone into the Rattlesnake area the day before, and he indicated to the press that this was the black female—the wolf that showed up behind Newman's apple tree. But Newman describes *her* wolf as being gray, despite the radio signals showing there was a black wolf in her orchard, not a gray one (according to Harms).

"She was big and gray with reddish tips on the end of her tail. And she had great big beautiful gray ears," Newman said.

The Marion female was as black as wet coal, from nose to tail, except for her green eyes; there couldn't have been that big a mistake.

"I kept talking to her the whole time, and she kept looking at me and my dogs," Newman said. "Then she just moseyed along."

Once the alpha female was down near Missoula, the way for her to get back to Marion would be to turn back west, rather than continuing on south and east toward Yellowstone. West would also take her toward central Idaho, where many wolves have been reported, though never (except for one dead one) verified until 1992. This is what she did, moving back north and west, crossing over into the Ninemile Valley, and there the black alpha female found what biologists had not been able to: another wolf in Montana, outside of the national park, a lone wolf that had probably come over from Idaho. Was it Irene Newman's "she" wolf? Perhaps; if it was indeed yet another wolf, and not a big coyote. At any rate, the black female found this big gray male, and they mated.

No one knows for sure what drew the female to the big male in the Ninemile Valley. She could have heard his howls on the wind—researchers say that howls can be heard by humans at distances up to four, sometimes even five or six miles, and there's no real telling at what distance other wolves can hear each other, or at what distances they can pick up their own species' scent. The encouraging thing about the Ninemile male was that he just appeared. It makes me think that even if one wolf got down to Yellowstone, others would then find it. Wolves have a lovely way of coming out of the woodwork, when game populations are high and winters are mild.

One thing that's strange and wonderful about the species is the way they go for one extra-long trip before settling down to den in April. They often go farther on these road trips than they've ever been before. Biologists who tell you on the one hand not to anthropomorphize will turn right around and state flatly that the wolves know they're going to be cooped up with the pups and want to go for one last adventure.

The Ninemile née Marion female was no exception: On March 30th, 1990, a pilot picked up her signal and found her all the way over near Lolo Pass with—and this is more encouragement in a story that, at times, needs it—*two* other wolves.

The male and female finished their adventure, came back home to the Ninemile, dug the den near a field owned by two ranchers, Ralph and Bruce Thisted, and settled in to give birth. The third wolf wasn't seen again.

It was a small pack—just the two adults, and then in April, six pups (three gray and three black). The male hunted whitetail fawns and dragged them back to the den while the mother stayed with the pups. In a larger, more complex pack, there are often aunts and sometimes uncles who baby-sit for the mother so she can get out of the den, and other pack members will help bring down game. It's a dangerous business, hunting—wolves often sustain broken ribs and cracked skulls while dragging down adult ungulates. It's one of the hideous, lovely dances of nature, the way the young newborn ungulates are easy to catch—how in the spring, when predators need extra food for their young, the woods are alive with soft, easy prey. Of course it's sad. I've heard that in parts of Canada, moose have evolved so that all the mothers drop their calves within twenty-four to forty-eight hours of each other—every moose mother in the forest dropping her calf, like acorns falling during a high wind, so that *some* calf survival is ensured. The sheer logistics save, by luck and chance, 60 percent of the calves, because while the wolves are busy gorging on this windfall of baby moose, there's not enough time to go around and catch them all, and by that third day, the baby moose are good runners. The moose population's future (and therefore the wolves') is protected.

The wolf-pack members can rarely afford hunting-sustained injuries, especially when there are pups to feed. It's a fine system, as long as you're not one of the baby moose that get caught, or one of the spotted fawns. The fawns are easier to drag back to the den. Of course, any one of those male spotted fawns might have grown up to become antlered bucks, which then might have wandered across the cross hairs of some rich out-of-state hunter's rifle scope, thereby capitulating the various and related direct and indirect influx of moneys into the state's economy. But there are too many deer, record numbers of deer—neither the state nor the hunters should fear competition, nor should economics enter a matter of law ("but he murdered a *poor* man, Judge . . .").

There is a debt to be paid, and it is in the wolf's favor. We owe the wolf a huge payment for the misery we exacted in developing and taming the dry rangelands of the West into dusty factories of meat.

The other thing biologists—some biologists—tell you to watch out for, besides putting desired human traits on wolves, is symbolism. Joe Fontaine, another of the USF&WS biologists working the northern Rockies, warns, "Don't make the wolf bear your burden." Renée Askins, head of the Wolf Fund in Moose, Wyoming, praises the symbolism not of wolves, but of the wolf's return, and airs specifically her hopes for the return of the wolf to Yellowstone. Askins, who has a doctorate in biology from Yale, once raised captive pups in Michigan and has never been the same; that was twenty-one years ago.

"Reintroducing wolves to Yellowstone is an act of making room, of giving up the notion of 'bigger, better, and more,' to hold onto 'complete, balanced, and whole,'" Askins writes. "It is an act of giving back, a realigning, a recognition that we make ecological and ethical mistakes and learn from them, and what we learn can inform our actions. Thus reintroducing wolves to Yellowstone is a symbolic act just as exterminating wolves from the West was a symbolic act," says Askins.

But we have drifted off the scent. Wolves eat fawns in the spring and early summer. There are too many deer in the Ninemile Valley—way too many. In the absence of natural predators, it may be argued, *any* deer are too many. By selecting so heavy-handedly for deer and against predators, we have disrupted the amplitudes of the natural rise-and-fall cycles of both predators and prey, so that now we see only the rise-rise-rise cycle.

Things were working real nice in the Ninemile Valley for the mother and father wolf and the six pups. None of that Marion trauma. Sometimes the cows would watch the mother and her pups play at the edge of the cows' meadow.

What you may think is coming did not come. The wolves did not bother the cows.

Sometimes, when the mother and father wolf—the alphas— and their pack head off on their end-of-March, first-of-April "last flings," the females don't make it back to the den in time to give birth. John Murray, a writer in Alaska, tells about one alpha female in Denali National Park who was trotting home from one such trip and who had to stop and give birth out in the middle of the tundra—had to lie down in just a small depression out of the wind. It was twenty-four hours before she could move the pups to her real den, so in the meantime the rest of the pack brought her snowshoe hares and stood guard to protect her and the pups from any wandering-by grizzlies. It's a lovely story, and so close to our own species' Christmas story that I feel a most unscientific empathy . . .

June 10th, 1990, was the last time anyone saw the Ninemile female alive. One of the Thisted brothers—the two old ranchers who observed the wolves at length—saw the mother sitting at the edge of their meadow with the pups swarming her, licking her.

On July 4th, a fisherman found her collar floating in the Nine-mile River. It had been cut and thrown from the bridge. By all indications, the rarest of things had been killed: A "good" wolf that would have nothing to do with cows. She had probably had nothing to do with the killings up in Marion—that had been almost certainly the coyotes, or the old tooth-worn male, who had had to do the hunting for her while she stayed in the den with those first ill-fated pups. She would have been a good mother, would have been a fine example to her new pups about how not to bring down cows, and we miss her. I miss her.

The principal business in the Ninemile Valley is wintering cattle and providing spring birthing grounds before turning the cows out onto the surrounding federal lands for summer grazing. It's been that way for a long time. It's just like almost every small valley in Montana. The big gray male, the loner, was left to raise the pups by himself. I remember reading about it in the newspaper almost every day that summer. The sadness of the female's absence lingered. She was gone, but hard to forget.

THREE

In talking about how a wolf pack will seek out the weak and the lame whenever possible—choosing the prey that is least likely to injure the pack in a fight—a cold-blooded logic is implied, the ruthless machinery of hunger. This is not always the case.

Wolves are so full of passion that they can barely stand it. That same summer that the widowed Ninemile male was dragging fawns back to his family's den, a wolf pack up in Alaska hunted down four grizzlies—a mother and three yearling cubs—because the grizzlies had wandered too close to the wolves' den. Normally, grizzlies dominate wolves; they'll run them off a carcass and claim the spoils, draping their whole body across the carcass like a basketball player claiming a much valued rebound. Grizzlies will even eat wolves when they can catch and kill them.

But not this time. The wolf pack in Denali (twelve hunting members) was pissed because the grizzlies had crossed that boundary of motherhood, had come far too close to the den, and the very next day, the wolves *sanctioned* the grizzlies: went out hunting, caught up with the bears and killed two of the young grizzlies and wounded the other young bear and the big sow. There weren't any second chances, no bluffing the way two species capable of hurting each other usually do; nor was there the discipline, or desire, on the wolves' part, to serve their revenge "cold," as the Sicilian adage goes. There was too much passion. The wolves were last seen by a park biologist carrying grizzly-bear body parts back to their den for their pups to feed on.

Some dry biologist might say, "Oh, that's just a selective advantage, same as preying on the weak—the pack's pups *must* be preserved at all costs, for they are the pack's future—and it's a selective advantage for a population to enforce aggressively its home territory, especially during the denning season"—but the wolves endured all kinds of wounds in their battle with the grizzlies, and it's nature's design to try and avoid lacerations, broken bones, infections, death. I think that evolutionary stuff is fine up to a point, but that there is also a point where it becomes bullshit—that twelve wolves attacking and fighting *to the death* four grizzlies is pure passion, revenge and nothing else.

Ninemile. I need to stick to that one small skinny valley in northwest Montana. But it is not one story. All wolves are tied together. It's a brotherhood, a sisterhood. You can't help it. They—the wolves—remind us of ourselves on our better days, our best days. They teach us splendidly about the overriding force of nature, too—about the way we've managed to suppress and ignore it in ourselves, or judge it.

One of the not-nice things wolves do is wage war on dogs. It's deadly business, this sometimes-fine balance between deer (or moose or elk) numbers and wolf numbers, and it just won't do, to the wolves' way of thinking, to have other wild dogs or coyotes roaming the woods, chasing down deer, and doing it much more sloppily, inefficiently—*terrorizing* the deer herds with long, fruitless chases. Wolf chases in northwest Montana, says Mike Jimenez, are usually pretty short—so short that when it's over, the rest of the deer herd, in the winter, may move off only another couple hundred yards and then look back, watching with dull interest as the pack settles in to feast (they eat the entrails first; the easiest meat goes first, fastest). Barry Lopez wrote, in *Of Wolves and Men*, of the "bystander phenomenon," as discussed by the naturalist Douglas Pimlott. "Two prey animals are pursued," Lopez writes, "and while wolves focus on one the other backtracks to watch its companion killed."

Coyotes usually fare poorly when wolves are able to establish themselves in a valley. USF&WS biologist Joe Fontaine says that ranchers for that reason alone should *welcome* wolves. Being so much warier of humans, wolves pose nowhere near the livestock threat that coyotes do, and wolves can keep coyote populations lower than any government trapper.

Wolves kill dogs with a passion. Sometimes they just kill them, but other times they eat them. Biologists speak again of that "search image." Next to livestock, the dog—the family pet—is the species that comes off most poorly when the wolf's search image gets skewed from its usual ungulate. And—so the theory goes—once *one* interloper dog is killed, the killing plants that new search image in the wolf's brain; the wolf begins to hunt dogs, to seek them.

There could be some more of that famous wolf passion implicated in the act. Many of the documented dog mass murders have taken place in August, as do most of the violent crimes among our own passionate species. Again, the biologists scoff at such musings, but the numbers are there.

This is not to say that wolves will not kill dogs the other eleven months of the year. On April 20th, 1990, for instance—about the time that the black female was giving birth to her six pups—the Ninemile male went out and fought with two dogs in their owner's yard, injuring both of them.

Wolves have been especially brutal on dogs in Minnesota. Steve Fritts, who used to work there, has a fine story about one wolf in northern Minnesota who came into a backyard, killed the dog that was chained to its doghouse, ate the dog (a chow), and then, as if to express its passion with less ambiguity, dragged the doghouse a quarter of a mile into the woods, where the wolf then chewed on *that*.

In Minnesota, about half of all reported wolf–dog conflicts ended with the dog surviving, and the dog-killing wolf packs seemed to have no correlation at all to the "bad" wolves that bothered livestock: only four of the forty-seven complaints about wolves fighting dogs had any association with concurrent live-stock attacks. The wolves were strictly after dogs. Wolves killed dogs ranging in size from a miniature poodle (yea!) to a Norwegian elkhound. Steve Fritts and Bill Paul write in their monograph, "Interactions of Wolves and Dogs in Minnesota," that "based on our investigations and interviews with dog owners, we believe that small- to medium-sized dogs, which may be particularly excitable and vocal, are more likely to provoke attack by wolves . . .

"In several incidents . . . wolves evidently focused their attention on dogs so intently that they were almost oblivious to buildings and humans. Most wolf attacks on dogs . . . occurred in the property-owners' yards and, with only two exceptions, within one hundred meters of the owners' house. In one case, a wolf attacked a dog near the doorstep and would not retreat until beaten with a shovel."

It often happens just by chance. A lone wolf (though sometimes the whole pack) is out wandering, and comes across a dog. Though the West is ripe with stories of dog–wolf liaisons, such tales almost always take place around an abnormal social situation: a lone, older wolf, lonely (passion!) and weakening, or a wolf in captivity.

After the Ninemile female was shot in June, the male took over raising the pups by himself. Despite the fact that up to half of the $100,000 fine can go to whoever provides information leading to a conviction for the killer of an endangered species, the Ninemile female's murderer has not yet been caught. I think what a startling amount of our own hateful passion—$100,000, and a year's worth of jail—it must take to pull the trigger on one wolf, and of how that wolf's killer must be haunted by the fear of someone turning him in for a half share. It's either an incredible amount of passion on the human side of the equation, or an incredible amount of stupidity and ignorance.

The big male brought white-tailed deer and elk pieces to his pups. The male and the six pups were seen regularly in the company of livestock, but no livestock was ever killed.

"He's a model dad," Ed Bangs said. The whole state was starting to get a warm feeling about the goings-on. It was all just a little too *neat*. It was like—well, like they were our pets. Bangs's passion flared once again, and he could have been speaking for a large percentage of the state when he said, "I would like to get the person who shot the female wolf and wring his neck."

Watching the whole scene, from start to finish, were the two

Thisted brothers—Ralph and Bruce. They had a beautiful big bay window facing due west, looking down on their pasture beneath the magnificent visage of Squaw Peak—forested green mountains up at the end of a heavily timbered canyon, capped with white cirques—and it was in their tall-grass pasture that the wolves chose to play, and to use as a rendezvous site.

The two brothers—they've ranched the Ninemile for over fifty years now—got a spotting scope, and then a video camera. They watched the wolves almost constantly.

"I could watch them forever," Bruce said. Ralph, an athletic sixty-plus years old (he and Bruce once pushed my rental car out of a snowdrift), said he'd seen wolf tracks (probably the male's) behind the house while out cross-country skiing in January of that year and had reported them, though at the time no one had paid any attention: just another rumor.

The big male continued to bring the pups out into the field to play and chase mice. Things seemed *static*.

But in August—the hot, dog-killing month—the big male crossed some invisible line that only humans could see. He was moving the six pups to a moose calf he'd killed by himself (it was too heavy and too far away to drag all the way to the pups) and he encountered a dog at a residence in the valley. The dog belonged to a woman named Shirley, who loved the old dog—Bear—very much. I'd like to theorize that Bear, a thirteen-and-a-half-year-old German shepherd, started hassling the male wolf and his pups, but this may not have been the case. Shirley and her husband—ranchers, but wolf supporters (at the time)—drove up and caught the final throes of the battle in their headlights, in their own driveway. The incident, regrettably, changed their thinking about wolves in the valley, though since then, the

USF&WS biologists have been "bending over backwards" to help Shirley keep an eye on her cattle, and the biologists—Fontaine, Fritts, Bangs and Jimenez—are genuinely pained about the incident. I can tell they feel responsible, as if it's their fault, as if it's something *they've* done . . . (Logging trucks have killed dozens of dogs as well as cattle in the Ninemile, thundering up and down the narrow gravel road, but they can't be held accountable, it seems; trucks, unlike wolves, are not judged.)

The whole state of Montana kept getting closer and closer to these wolves. Well, almost the whole state. Up in Kalispell, the local archery shop was selling baseball caps that said "Wolf Management Team" and had on the caps the picture of a gray wolf seen through the cross hairs of a rifle scope. And the state officials seemed to be feeling less than warm about the deer-eating sons-of-bitches. But everyone else was interested, willing to give the wolves a chance, as if believing that we, the humans, had some moral authority to make that choice.

FOUR

There are short stories, and then there are long ones. This one is already set firmly into the latter category—*all* must be told—so while we're speaking of moral authority, of our *debt* to the wolves, it strikes me that this is the time to tell how the Native Americans felt toward the wolf-getters of the late 1800s. This is a long, long history, but there is nothing wrong with knowing all of the facts—*all* of them. I'm tired of representations, quick-grasp surface pictures. This is all there is, this is all I've heard. If you give the wolves just a little space, and one or two, or two or three mild winters, they just might make it.

The easiest way to kill wolves in the nineteenth century was with strychnine, and it was used from Mexico up through Texas, and all the way into the Arctic. Stanley Young, an old government wolf-getter, tells how Joseph Taylor wrote in his 1891 book, *Twenty Years on the Trap Line*, that "poisoned wolves and foxes in their dying fits often slobber upon the grass, which becoming sun dried holds its poisonous properties a long time, often causing the death months or even years after of the pony, antelope, buffalo, or animals feeding upon it. The Indians losing their stock in this way feel like making reprisals, and often did."

Bully for them. The wolf-getters got the wolves (and ponies, antelope, and buffalo), and the Indians got the wolf-getters. They just didn't get enough of them.

Young tells in his book, *The Last of the Loners*, how buffalo-hunters and wolf-trappers in Kansas in the 1870s had paved a road with gray-wolf bones and carcasses. The torturing and maiming of wolves is listed in great and stunning detail in Barry Lopez's *Of Wolves and Men*—setting live wolves on fire is the method that gets to me the most. Torture seems to have been a cultural phenomenon that's vanished, other than poisoning, which continues with vigor down in Mexico and up in Canada, and is one reason the Mexican wolf has been unable to repopulate the southwestern United States.

In 1861, three wolf-getters took more than three thousand wolves, coyotes and foxes (the entire kill netting them $2500). Songbirds—larks—were killed for bait and laced with strychnine and then scattered like candy along known wolf runways. It became an unwritten rule of the range for ranchers to carry poison in their saddlebags and never pass up a carcass of any kind without injecting it with strychnine.

The results were always the same. "They would kill a buffalo and cut the meat in small pieces," William E. Webb wrote in 1872, "which were scattered in all directions, a half mile or so from camp, and so bait the wolves for about two days . . . Meanwhile all hands were preparing meat in pieces about two inches square . . . putting a quantity of strychnine in the center. One morning after putting out the poison they picked up sixty-four wolves, and none of them over a mile and a half from camp."

Sixty-four wolves, in a morning—at the bait-inspired conflu-
ence of two? three? four packs? The pack sizes were larger then,
out on the plains, to cut buffalo out of the great herds. That size
of wolf pack won't ever be seen again, unless the buffalo herds
return.

I picture a mile-wide circle of dying wolves, the prairie writh-
ing with them in the moonlight as they flop and back-flip in their
slow, agonized deaths.

Taylor writes again about the wolf-getter of the 1870s: "If it
was in the autumn he moved slowly in the wake of a buffalo herd
. . . shooting down a few of the beasts . . . After ripping them
open, saturating their warm blood and intestines with from one
to three bottles of strychnine to each carcass . . . he makes a camp
in a ravine or coulee and prepares for the morrow.

"With the first glimmer of light in the eastern sky he rises,
makes his fire, and cooks his coffee, then hitches up . . . and follows his [trap] line to the finish. Around each buffalo carcass will
probably be from three to a dozen dead wolves."

FIVE

The Ninemile landowners were "great," Mike Jimenez says. He's been in charge of following the Ninemile pack for their whole history, for two generations, going on a third—and I like him. He has little guile about him—unusual, I think, for a G-man—and he's consumed by the wolves. He's got that passion to match theirs. Sherry Devlin, who reported daily on the wolves' status in the *Missoulian*, praises Jimenez's untiring efforts to answer all reporters' questions at all hours of the day. The phone's always ringing at Jimenez's house, and no matter how tired he is, he answers the phone—another stranger calling, wanting to know the whole story, from start to finish, in twenty-five words or less. But always, Jimenez's voice grows light, he becomes more affable than ever, and begins updating the pack's situation as if they are—and there's no way around this cliché—his children. He's black-haired, dark-eyed, athletic, and smallish, looking much younger than his forty-five years. A fine surrogate father for wolves.

Jimenez had had rough luck with wolves before. He spent two years up in the Wigwam Flats area of British Columbia, where one of the two packs in the area, the Headwaters Pack, was poisoned; five of their ten members were found dead, and only the alpha female was known for sure to have survived—those enduring, strong, alpha-mothers—to cross over from British Columbia into Alberta.

The other pack in Jimenez's Wigwam Flats area was called the Wigwam Pack, and it too had disappeared a year before. Jimenez had never been able to figure out why, though poisoning was suspected there, as well. The Wigwam Pack went from eight wolves in the winter to only one wolf (possibly two) in the summer. Jimenez tracked those remaining wolves the next winter (1989–1990) and determined there were only two wolves hanging on in the entire historical area; once great Wigwam Flats was swimming in bad medicine, with seventeen of nineteen wolves from two packs gone in a year, probably from poison.

"I did my master's degree on these two packs and spent two years in the field following these wolves," Jimenez says, "so you can imagine what a bummer these continual 'disappearing' and dead wolves are."

After the gray male's scrap with Bear, the German shepherd, in August, there weren't any more problems—none confirmed, anyway. A couple of other dogs disappeared, but that happens all the time in the country.

The male spent the last three weeks of his life playing in the meadow with his pups, chasing them and showing them how to hunt mice. It was still too early to take them on a trip, to chase deer with them, to show them how to kill. That would come in September and October, when the pups had their real teeth. In August they still had their "milk" teeth and it would be another month or two before they could begin to keep up with the male on a real hunt.

Wolf pups grow quickly, though not quite as fast as the growth rate of their prey species; the prey's got to maintain some kind of advantage, a head start. By the age of four months, pups' feet already measure four and a half inches across; at full maturity, they'll have only increased another inch and a half. David Mech writes that "in the field they look like adults by late fall," and Diane Boyd, who's been following the wolves up in Glacier for almost twenty years, writes that "it is impossible" to distinguish a late-year pup from an adult.

At maturity, wolves can stand as tall as three feet, *at the shoulders*, though they average between twenty-six and thirty-two inches, and from tip of nose to end of tail measure between five and six and a half feet long, with the males usually being half a foot longer than the females. With a length of six feet, we're not talking about coyotes.

Wolves can reach speeds of between thirty-five and forty miles per hour, and have been seen to "bound tremendously when pursuing moose and deer," Mech writes. Some bounds have been measured at sixteen feet.

The westbound section of Interstate 90 that crosses the Ninemile River, heading to Idaho, isn't sixteen feet; it's wider, and on September 1st, 1990, a large dog was reported killed on the interstate near the river crossing—a large gray dog.

The wolf—the Ninemile male—was picked up at daylight. I've seen the photographs of him there on the side of the road, and he was pretty mashed up. It's odd to see that motionlessness imposed upon an animal whose existence is tied to the fact that it never stops moving. When I exclaimed to Jimenez about the apparent shortness of the wolf's muzzle—a possible indication that he might not be pure wolf—Jimenez said that had been his same thought, looking at the photo, but then when he looked at the wolf's body, he realized that none of the body parts were their proper length or size after the accident—that the wolf had had to be kind of rearranged, before being photographed there on the side of the road.

For the next three nights, Jimenez went out to the Thisteds' pasture and howled.

The pups howled back with great eagerness—"It was like, Dad's back!" is how Jimenez described their answers—and the feds scrambled, trying to decide what to do: the memory of the previous litter's starvation in Glacier still rang in their minds. The last thing they wanted to do was *touch* the wolves, if they could help it. Soon, if they kept touching, they would have nothing left to study, nothing left to recover.

"We're going to lose some," Ed Bangs said, preparing people for the worst, and there was much philosophical talk about "that's nature," and, shrugging, "Some make it in the wild, some don't."

I believed none of it. These guys act and preach automation and data (all except Jimenez and a few others), but they're in it for the same reasons we are—for the passion. Even Ed Bangs, a dyed-in-the-wool longtime G-man, laces his position papers with poetic excerpts such as "To regret deeply is to live afresh" (Thoreau), and labels the problem that arose between humans and wolves as conflicts between "what were once 'brothers in the hunt.'"

Bangs goes on to give the standard biologists' patter to caution "younger, primarily urban residents" against loving wolves for "having desirable human traits such as being caring parents, loving mates." But it's no good—when Bangs starts quoting Thoreau, he can't hide his poet's heart beating wildly just beneath the fine print of even his *technical* papers, his monographs.

The USF&WS took the state agency—the MDFWP—into their confidence and discussed the idea of feeding the pups. The upside of the situation was that it would allow the pups to survive; six weeks of feeding was the estimated time necessary to "launch" the pups into hunting adulthood. The biologists would drop dead game animals at the pups' rendezvous site and would be able to determine once and for all if there was another adult lingering on the pups' outside territory. Another advantage of supplemental feeding was that the pups would probably stay in their home meadows—a secure location where they had not, and therefore probably would not, bother livestock.

The Thisted brothers were delighted: They would get to watch the wolves some more. Bangs wrote, in his official position paper, "At their present location they are closely monitored by the cooperative landowner, and most local residents are supportive of these wolves." The MDFWP, however, "indicated they were not supportive of a long-term feeding program for the pups while the situation was evaluated," Bangs wrote. "They did not support killing deer to feed the pups."

Road-killed deer, yes, said the state, *for a while*—speaking as if they, and not the feds, had authority with endangered species. But no *live* deer. No deer "harvested."

The downside—and everybody was aware of this, it was like walking on eggs—was that a pack of tame wolves might be raised in the middle of cow country.

On the 4th of September, 1990, Mike Jimenez put two road-killed deer out at the rendezvous site, and then a third the next day. The Thisteds gave their okay for the wolves to stay on their property as long as no livestock was lost.

Because the pups couldn't even bite through the deers' hides to eat them, Jimenez first opened all the deers' bellies with a knife. The game plan was to feed the pups deer (trying to keep the carcass free of human scent) until the start of hunting season—late October—at which point wounded deer, gut-shot and butt-shot "mistakes" by the hunters, were expected to be staggering around the woods, creating a sudden increase in the availability of easy prey. There would be gut-piles in the woods too, huge mounds of blood and entrails where the more successful hunters found and then field-dressed their deer.

In theory, the wolves would have no problem finding dead animals, because carrion's presence is broadcast widely by the ravens and magpies in the valley. But no one knew if the wolves would be able to figure that out—or if they would know it by instinct. The wolves would have their sense of smell to find carrion. The big question was: Would they be able to teach themselves to hunt, to find and bring down healthy animals? There weren't any cases on record of orphan pups ever surviving. Orphan human beings being raised by wolves and surviving, yes, but no orphan wolves making it in the wild—whether on their own or with the help of humans.

On September 6th, the USF&WS received a letter from the MDFWP recommending that the feds not feed the pups—a 180-degree change in position over the course of only twenty-four hours—precisely the kind of volatility in management that Joe Fontaine has warned against and which can be characteristic of politically appointed agencies. The state recommended that the pups instead be captured, fed in captivity, as was done with the pups' half sisters the year before up in Marion, the ones that starved to death—and then to make a "soft" release in—and I wonder what they had in mind—"a national park where wolves already exist."

Once again, the state was trying to get wolves out of an area where people hunted deer; which is to say, 99 percent of Montana.

The state further indicated, wrote Bangs, "that if the Service decides to feed the wolf pups at their present location, we [the feds] must (1) accept liability for any subsequent depredations," and "(2) obtain deer from federal facilities where hunting is not allowed and surplus animals are available." K. L. Cool, director of the MDFWP, went straight to the problem as he saw it and said, additionally, that he wanted the wolf taken off the endangered species list.

"Wolves have the capacity to dramatically affect hunter opportunities in this state," Cool said. "They should not automatically win out over game animals."

The remark about how they should be taken off the endangered species list intrigued me.

The position of the state of Montana regarding wolves is that MDFWP has "recovered all the wildlife species that are residents of the state." I don't know exactly what they mean by this statement, because the gray wolf has not recovered, nor has the giant white sturgeon (there are maybe six of them left in the whole state), nor giant paddlefish (dams are doing in both sturgeon and paddlefish), nor woodland caribou, nor harlequin ducks, and perhaps not the great gray owl (no figures are available for it). Martens? No. Fishers? Hell, no. What about the red-backed vole, the shy creature that helps, through tunneling, spread truffle pores in old-growth forests? The last time I checked—yesterday—it, too, was still on the endangered species list.

The state wants management control of wolves, and a flexibility in that management, they say, that "means killing [the wolf] where it isn't compatible with 'the program,' and encouraging it where it is."

And it means, too, withholding the state's road-killed deer in a childish game of tit for tat: trying to *extort* the feds, it seems, into killing, or moving those pups.

The problem MDFWP has with the Endangered Species Act is that they feel it means wolves get to live anywhere they please. The state has argued that neither grizzlies nor wolves are threatened or endangered (their respective federal listings in Montana) because there are plenty of wolves and grizzlies in Alaska and Canada. This Reaganesque method of enumeration is several decades out of date, paying no attention whatsoever to the simple concept of ecosystems, bioregions, or life. Up until last year, the MDFWP allowed a limited hunting season on grizzlies in Montana (though a federal lawsuit in the fall of 1991 finally stopped it). This attitude of fear and aggression comes straight from the top—the state agency—and tries to work its way down through the net.

The wolves, as ever, keep running.

Who should control an endangered species—before (if) it recovers? I don't trust the state and its juggernaut of power, once set in motion.

I *like* the accountability the feds have, on federal lands—how they're accountable to the nation, not just to a few local voters. Joe Fontaine says it well.

"Wildlife doesn't do well when it's subjected to the changing volatility of state politics, that change in political influence, especially in a small state. We just lost a national representative due to the population changes."

"The guys he's dealing with," Mike Jimenez says—speaking of the governor's backers—"have a lot of power. He's responsible to that." We're in a restaurant, drinking coffee, not far from where the pups live. Mike's kind of looking off into the distance. One of the things that impresses me about the feds is that they understand the politics of the situation every bit as well as they do the biology. This is a sloppy generalization, but I think it's why they are where they are: that if all they wanted to focus on was wolf biology, and wolf ecology—*solely*—then they'd be with a university somewhere, doing research, studying only wolves and ignoring people. And if all they wanted to focus on was people and politics, they'd be in some higher echelon of state government—directors of the MDFWP, maybe. They're working in the middle of the weave. They've got to have a broader scope; they understand both aspects, perhaps as completely as the aspects can be understood.

They're G-men.

Jimenez, with the energy that characterizes him, scrambled, looking for road-killed deer to feed the pups before the state pulled the permit they'd issued allowing him to use road kills. The pups, whether Jimenez realized it or not, weren't the feds' pups, or the state's pups, but rather were becoming *his*, in the way that when your heart belongs to something, that thing then it belongs to you, or more correctly, you belong to it.

"It was tough," Jimenez says. "I was driving fifty, sixty miles a night, up and down the roads, looking, hoping someone had hit a deer . . ."

While the MDFWP was unwilling to baby-sit the pups, the state's residents were more than willing. The response from citizens, Ed Bangs said, was "amazing." One woman offered to donate her year's supply of venison, straight out of the freezer. Another said she had "a lot of old chickens." One man asked if he could set up a guard station in the valley, to watch over and protect the pups.

Bangs tactfully turned down all offers. Wolves, politics and people were now fully meshed in the net, and watching over the whole seat-of-the-pants efforts were the two brothers, living up at the far end of the valley, the last year-round residents at the northern end of the valley.

They're the damnedest ranchers I've ever met. They've got the attitude toward nature that you usually see only in the movies, or in a few extremely old Zen priests: an acceptance of boundaries, and of the knowledge that not all of nature can be controlled. Maybe the wolves sought them out.

Whatever the Thisteds' philosophy, it's clear they enjoyed having the wolf pups in their pasture. They've got that huge bay window, and below their house, the pasture, and then the woods, and the river, and beyond that, the great mythic-looking mountain. Ralph would climb up into the loft of their barn nearly every morning, in the summer and early fall, and film the pups' antics with his video camera. He'd film Mike's antics, too; Jimenez has the ingenuity and enthusiasm of a boy—the *passion*—to go along with his expertise and his political cool, keeping his head down, alert and aware of the net above him, all around him, but doing his work. Jimenez had struck upon an inspired idea for locating the necessary road kills. He asked bicyclists where to find the deer, which were often by that point smelly and large. Motorists, Jimenez reasoned, whiz past everything, but *cyclists* bear witness to the road-killed deer—and so Jimenez was able to stay up with, if not ahead of, the young wolves' appetites.

The MDFWP was in *anguish*, in the meantime, lamenting that these road-killed deer had "car smell" on them. The feds—

Joe Fontaine and Jimenez—raised their eyebrows when I aired this objection, though Fontaine did say that wolves don't yet have a search image for trucks or cars.

Jimenez was improvising like mad. He'd drag the road kill out to the rendezvous site when the wolves were on the other side of the valley, and he wore gloves to try and keep his scent off the carcass. After the wolves began warming to his prepared meals, he tried to stay ahead of their fast-developing minds by spreading the carcasses out in various orientations, even going so far as to prop the dead deer up in a running position so that the wolves would get the idea that they were to attack from behind; that life in the wild would not always consist of walking up to a prepared, belly-up, leg-splayed, fat waiting buck, every hour on the hour.

Sometimes, up in his barn's loft, waiting for daylight, Ralph's hands would get so cold that he'd shake violently, and sometimes the video reflects his cold-shaking, though other times it is quite excellent. "I wish I had it to do over again," Ralph says, now that the pups are grown and gone, "and knew more about running a camera. It was dark when we'd set up the camera. Cold," he says.

Sometimes Ralph would film a black object at the edge of his pasture for long minutes at a time, right at daylight, his eyes blurring in the cold, before the lengthening light finally revealed the object to be a charred stump.

But when the camera's on the wolves, there's no mistaking them. They're delightful; they're nothing but puppies, rolling and playing with each other. They play king-of-the-mountain on a huge stump. One wolf runs around behind the stump, staring up at the god-puppy, clearly awed. The god-puppy leaps down on his or her sister or brother, establishing some kind of mega-dominance—not the usual roll-over, tail-tucked puppy dominance that the young wolves fart around with in the early days, but a great slam dunk from heaven—and then the two wolves play tag, around and around the stump. But the god-puppy never climbs up on the stump when the other one is in a position to see how it is done; he, or she, was clearly keeping that little hidden step-up on the back of the stump a secret.

There was another puppy that spent more time chasing the fluttering black-and-white magpies away from the carcass at the rendezvous site than he or she spent at the trough—clearly a dreamer, a taker-for-granted, perhaps, of these halcyon days.

"I called"—Ralph blushes, corrects himself—"*they* called that one Puppy," he says, almost shyly. "Anytime there was a bird flying by, it would chase it. Or a mouse—it was always tossing the mouse up, eating it."

The video shows one little black wolf—Puppy himself, or herself—always staying away from the other five, a loner already. And then Puppy disappeared, as did one of the gray puppies, into the deeper weave of the net. Either they made it (there have since been reports of a lone black wolf over near Alberton, Montana, just a valley away)—or they didn't. A mountain lion could have gotten them. Black bear. Grizzly bear. Anything. Or nothing.

Black bears kept dragging the road-killed deer from the middle of the pasture. Jimenez found that he had to chain the carcasses to a log, and then to a pipe he drove into the ground. Jimenez always carted off the leftover bones each time he brought in a new kill for the pups, and if the pups ever saw him, he'd fire a gun over their heads to frighten them away from his presence.

Jimenez dragged in a deer about every two or three days. When he couldn't find a road-killed deer—and up until the time the state pulled his road-kill gathering permit—he'd have to go over to the Lee Metcalf National Wildlife Refuge (federally owned and operated, like the national forests) and shoot a deer from some section of the refuge that was closed to public hunting. Perhaps it was a crafty ploy on the state's part to rouse hunters' outcry against the feds; whatever the case, it didn't work. People who wanted the wolves to survive understood certain measures would have to be taken. Again, there seemed to be some kind of invisible, crazy, zero-tolerance kowtowing going on between the MDFWP and Montana's hunters, who should have known better than anyone (for it's what they preach, with their talk of harvesting) the dangers of overpopulation.

The pups would lie out in the tall grass, in the high, thin autumn sun—the wind ruffling their long fur—and chase mice and grasshoppers, the same as they'd done when their parents were still living. And Jimenez kept dragging those carcasses in, trying to get them over the hump of adolescence.

Halcyon days, halcyon days.

There was still no indication in the least that the pups would ever be interested in doing anything other than lying in the sun, sleek and well rested, awaiting their next meal. That was the bad news.

The good news was that they weren't bothering any of the cows that were grazing all around them—sometimes within a few feet of them—as the wolves pursued their grasshoppers, or just lay there with the flattened grass warm on their bellies, gnawing on the dead deer's haunches.

"People are starting to trust us more," Joe Fontaine says when I mention that if the time came, the feds may have to kill a wolf that they can't trap, a wolf that might be killing a lot of cows; that the best thing for wolves in the Rockies indeed might be for that one individual to go, though not the whole pack. I make the understatement that "that's something a lot of people aren't going to understand or agree with."

"You bet," Mike and Joe say at the same time—laughing, then, at their simultaneity, and their shared dread of the future, of when that day arrives.

The backlash of *not* controlling wolf depredation on livestock, however, is what the feds really fear: Angry, vigilante ranchers, though small in number, can do the most harm; such ranchers are the ones who see the wolves in the woods first, and sometimes last. The thing the feds are most frightened of is poison. If ranchers feel there's no cooperation—if they get backed up against the wall, and feel like it's them against the world— then, says Fontaine, "They're going to solve the problem themselves. That's what they've done historically."

"If they do it [poison]," Fontaine says, "they're not going to care what else they take out with them, either. They're going to place some poisons out that are going to get a few individuals— indiscriminate killings—that will not only kill wolves, but they're going to kill eagles and grizzly bears and everything that eats meat.

"You need that credibility to develop in the ranching community," Fontaine says, "the credibility that we are going to *do* something, if there's depredation."

It's possible that this newly earned credibility—which began with the feds moving the wolves out of the Marion area the summer before when all the cow trouble started—has helped the increase in sightings that have been reported to the Fish & Wildlife Service. There are now confirmed sightings of wolves in the Yaak, in the Fortine–Tobacco Valley area, the Swan Valley, in the Little Belt Mountains and the Sapphire Mountains. The sightings usually involve lone disperser wolves, but there also have been several group sightings (unlike most of Idaho's rumors of wolves, 75 percent of which involve single animals). There are definitely wolves in Montana over on the other side of the Divide, near Choteau. "Tracks being cut like crazy," Jimenez says, though no one ever sees those wolves, just the tracks.

Doug Peacock, the grizzly bear expert, tells of how, in Europe, a handful of certain intelligent high-level predators such as wolves and grizzlies have adapted to special crowded situations, and of how they sleep all day and are active only at night. I think of that black Marion female, her whole *family* wiped out, struggling to keep the last genes alive, passing through the town of Bigfork, trotting down the sidewalks at night, perhaps; the radio-collar signals showed her going right past the little hydro-dam's powerhouse, there in the downtown area.

The wolf that's been rumored to be over in the Sapphire Mountains—if it's there—that's the one that could get to West Yellowstone. It'd be a cakewalk. In fact, it could be there now. There are rumors of wolves in the Beaverhead National Forest, too, just southwest of Dillon—closer still to Yellowstone country. There are even rumors beginning to come out of Yellowstone's interior. Any day, now, perhaps. Or not.

All through September, the Thisted brothers, who came to the Ninemile Valley fifty-four years ago, sat up on the hill in their house and watched the orphan pups from their big west-facing bay window, looking down on the field below. Just up the Ninemile canyon and over the summit lies the Thompson River valley and then one more summit, the rock and ice crags of the narrow Cabinet Mountains, and beyond that, Marion. It's strange to think that the wolf pups know nothing of that time or place, nor do there seem to be any wolves left who do; that last uncatchable pup back up in Marion had been killed in the spring, shot from a helicopter by Animal Damage Control officers after more calf predation occurred.

On the 25th of September, 1990, with hunting season less than a month away, Ed Bangs, Steve Fritts, Joe Fontaine and Mike Jimenez put out a trap line so that these Ninemile pups—like their beleaguered mother, and their Glacier-dead stepsisters the year before—could be collared. I don't mean to paint it as the kiss of death; it's just that, statistically, it seemed to lower their odds. A cloud passing across their sun. October coming, too, and then winter.

The good news for purists is that only two pups were captured. And maybe that's enough. Some wolves get roped in tight; others are sent skittering a little farther into the unknown, a little farther out of our reach. They caught a forty-three-pound black female pup—the image of her mother—on the second day of trapping, and a fifty-six-pound gray male pup (the image of his big father) on the fourth day.

The feds stopped the trapping then, to allow things to settle down, to keep from spooking the pack away from the rendezvous site—which the feds' reports now called, ominously, a "feeding station," which is, of course, what it had become—but after being collared and released, none of the pups, miraculously, left.

They did become wilder, much wilder. It's not so hard at all to catch a wolf that's never seen a trap before—this has always been the case, throughout the history of the West—but once pack members have seen one of their members caught in a trap, it gets much harder, almost impossible. If the Ninemile pack had to be captured again, it would probably have to be by helicopter and darts. Which would make them still wilder . . .

Ralph and Bruce Thisted seem to be in tight with Jimenez. They've been through a lot together. They've watched these pups grow up. Like junior gods, they've tried to care for the pups without the pups ever knowing that benevolent hands were hovering over them, just out of reach and sight. When I mention how Mike said he shot over the wolves' heads whenever he saw them, just to spook them, Bruce and Ralph say nothing, and their faces are like calm lake water: they give nothing. They know, I think, that the image of someone slinging hot lead in even the *general* direction of an endangered species might rile certain urban Eastern factions.

"To make them spooky," I say. "He was doing it to scare them. They seem a lot warier now."

Ralph relaxes. "Well, they were a lot spookier after they radio-collared them. I never got a picture, afterward. They never came out in the daytime—or even early morning, after they were radio-collared.

"They were over in the field—Papa Wolf with the pups. In July they stayed right out with the cattle."

Bruce cuts in. "I saw the male wolf right there by the mailbox." Bruce points out the bay window to the road. The mailbox is a stone's throw from the window. "He was long and rangy, he was awesome. It was a thrill."

"Fifty years," I say, marveling at that view of Squaw Peak, and the meadow and the river.

"Are you a bird-watcher?" Bruce asks, almost timidly.

"I don't know all their names," I say, "but I like to watch them, yes."

"Those are grosbeaks out there—with that yellow . . . "

"Wow!" I cry, peering straight down at all the birds hopping around at the base of a big ponderosa pine, right by that window.

I'd been staring off at the mountains, and off at where the wolves had been; I hadn't even noticed all the birds hopping around, pecking the seed that Bruce and Ralph had put out for them at the base of that big tree.

Ralph (proudly): "There's about fourteen or fifteen different species . . . Oh there's a thrush right there by the tree, at the base—he's been here about two weeks. I think maybe they're migrating through, probably for spring migration. There were two of 'em here this morning. Look right now, see, there's a siskin, and two kind of chickadees—and a thrush, and a junco . . ."

Bruce cuts in. "Blackbird around here, a little bit ago . . ."

Ralph's still counting: "Blue jay, or Stellar's jay . . ."

The big pine shades the whole north side of the house. We watch the birds for a while and then we look out once again at the meadow where the wolves used to feed and play. It is early March of 1991. Two of the pups are still unaccounted for—the little black one, Puppy, and the gray one—but four have made it for sure. The feds took a stand, a gamble, and it paid off. They won, this time.

Though really it was no gamble at all. They were just doing their job. They had to protect the species.

Back in October of 1990, on the 21st—the opening day of hunting season—the mood all through the USF&WS was one of barely staved-off fatalism. Everyone *knew* some hunter was going to shoot a wolf, either from meanness or thinking it was a coyote—not that coyote-shooting isn't its own act of meanness, but it's usually an unthinking, knee-jerk reaction for some people who find themselves suddenly in the woods or driving along a road with a gun within reach. There is no longer a culture of

66

wolf-killing. All the old wolf-killers are dead. There is only our strange hatefulness.

It was an all-or-nothing time for the biologists when gun season opened in October. The hunters would bring a vast and sudden wolf-windfall of crippled deer and elk, and gleaming pink gut-piles all through the woods, but also there would be a lot of honyocks with guns, a lot of honyocks cruising the roads slowly, looking for anything to kill. Having no specific search image. The crunch of gravel beneath their tires.

"They come through the backyard," Ralph said, speaking of these hunters, of which the Ninemile gets so many during the rifle season. "They walk right past the no trespassing sign and then yell at you if you step outside and try to say something to them."

"I'm glad when it's over," Bruce said.

"They shoot from the truck," Ralph said, "and if something runs off, they don't even go to check and see if they hit it—if they don't see it fall, they just drive on."

Last year Ralph walked a hundred yards down his road and found, in just that short distance, four deer and an elk that hunters had killed and left, and that was just in the ditch along his road. There's no telling how many cripples made it into the woods to die, out of sight to everyone except the ravens, magpies, and coyotes. And wolves.

In defense of the Ninemile hunters, I will say that I'm stereotyping a group—hunters—of which I am one, and which contains as much diversity as any other reviled minority. Ed Bangs reminded me that in the Ninemile, since the wolves showed up, "hunters have been really cooperative so far about reporting wolves and being open-minded about natural recovery." Pat Tucker of the National Wildlife Federation has pollings that show this to be no surprise: 71.5 percent of residents in north-western Montana were in favor of natural wolf recovery, as were nearly 60 percent of the hunters polled, as long as no restrictions were placed on hunters' limits of deer.

And I like to believe that the wolves are having a positive effect on hunters—that the hunters will be aware that they're now in the presence of far better hunters, and will try to act accordingly, will try to shoot straighter, for the neck perhaps, so that they either kill or miss, but do not wound, do not lose game, as Bruce and Ralph testify has been the case in the past . . .

"Hunters are a key component to recovery," Bangs reminded me. "They have the greatest opportunity to illegally kill wolves if they decide to and they are the best source for wolf observations.

"I have a motto," Bangs adds. "Don't piss off 200,000 people with guns, if they aren't doing anything wrong."

The roads were what bothered the biologists the most. "The wolf is a real habitual user of roads," said Joe Fontaine. "He uses it to hunt deer and to travel, but increased road density leads to increased vulnerability—poaching—of wolves."

Jimenez drove the roads all during the hunting season in his sea-green truck, stopping and talking to hunters, letting them know what the situation was. He placed caution signs in key areas, tried to maintain what the USF&WS called "a high pro-file," with intensive monitoring of the wolves' radio-collar signals to discourage either accidental or intentional killings. Even as late as October, Fritts, Fontaine and Ed Bangs were uttering phrases like "slim to none," "risky, at best," and "long shot" to describe the pups' chances. The state was still giving the feds a dose of grief—keeping up the pressure, like hounds baying at some prey's hindquarters, demanding from the feds on some days "fuller cooperation," and on other days, "complete control."

Glen Marx, the natural resources aide to Governor Stephens, said that state officials began to request full management right after "several Marion-area ranchers complained of wolf depredation [never proven] on livestock. Those wolves were relocated; all eventually died," the state complained.

It's a galling thing indeed to watch the state point fingers at the feds in that Marion debacle. I can't stress enough how much I respect the feds' cool, professional demeanor when the state starts nipping at them like this. In my mind, if blame had to be assigned in the Marion case, it would have to be placed on the state too, for bullying the federal biologists into a change-of-site for the relocation—one where a holding pen couldn't be constructed, where supplemental feeding couldn't be used, and where there was no game for the wandering, relocated pups.

But the feds simply smile with perhaps just the *edges* of beleaguerment showing, and go about their job and continue, patiently, to give the same answers: saying that the state's entry into wolf management is *welcomed*, saying that they are sympathetic to the state's concerns, but that first the wolf must be recovered.

Ed Bangs says that the state will be able to best manage the wolf "in the long run"—after the feds get it off the endangered species list.

But still the state won't back off; they push, and press. Before the federal lawsuit stopped the MDFWP's hunting season on grizzly bears, and shortly after the feds denied the state's request to let the state manage the wolves, the state announced—almost as if in revenge—that MDFWP was going to try to *increase* the grizzly bear "harvest."

Montana governor Stan Stephens said that the feds should stop their "unproductive hand-wringing and whimpering" about the grizzlies being threatened, and MDFWP director K. L. Cool added, "Our department finds it increasingly difficult to maintain a professional cooperative relationship . . . when the USF&WS cannot abide by its own rules and allows emotional hyperbole to supersede biologically sound and technically correct wildlife management"—sounding a little emotional himself, there.

Back to wolves. "The name-bashing," says Jimenez, "you don't get anywhere. And in the long run, wolves disappear. Over the years, you know, the name-bashing keeps going on, but the wolves just disappear. And so we don't make any progress."

Jimenez kept on driving the roads, talking to hunters. And when hunting season was over—late November—the wolves had made it through another layer of the weave. Several hunters reported *seeing* the wolves while out hunting, but Jimenez had done his job in advertising the need to protect the wolves, as had the ranchers, who, Jimenez says, were starting to get attached to the wolves in "a weird sort of way." They all had pictures of the wolves, Jimenez says, and they all knew when the wolves' howling schedule was, back when they were puppies.

"They don't mind a few wolves," Joe Fontaine says. "Most of them don't."

SIX

The only thing left for the pups to do, it seemed, was run that last gauntlet: to learn to kill.

The theory was that they'd find crippled deer at first, and chase them down, and teach themselves. The pups were starting to get bolder, though still not going off on the long, confident rambles that adult wolf packs love to make. They'd increased their range from one mile around the rendezvous site to three miles, and then, in late October, with hunters in the woods, to five miles, and then seven . . .

Snow, the field-biologist's currency, was falling. And Jimenez was in the woods, backtracking—checking to see where the wolves had been, and what they'd been doing—but always following the fresh tracks backward, to keep from stumbling upon the wolves and disturbing them. Moving through the woods on snowshoes. Why he took this job.

Back in late September, when two of the four Ninemile pups were caught and collared, Jimenez would sit up in the barn with the Thisteds and, as in a scene from *Miami Vice*, would use a night scope to observe the pups, who had begun returning to the rendezvous site, but only at night.

In the National Bison Range, near Moiese, Montana, two bighorn sheep died, and as it was a federal refuge, one where the state couldn't butt in and pull any permits, the USF&WS brought those sheep carcasses over to the rendezvous site, thinking: *fresh meat*.

But the pups were used to whitetails and wouldn't touch the sheep. They circled them repeatedly, and only nibbled on a small portion near one of the shoulders. This well-documented behavior of wolves shows the importance of the pack, of having parents to teach what's okay to eat and what's not. You'd think wolves would figure out what's meat—that *anything* is okay to eat—but they seem to be programmed genetically to follow very strict orders from their pack. Just as they use a search image, they seem to use feeding images, too. If they haven't seen their parents eat it—if they haven't developed a taste for it within the pack's confines—chances are fair they won't develop the taste for it out of the blue. The implications with regard to cattle depredation are obvious.

"After three days, the biologists dragged the sheep away and replaced it with a deer, which," wrote Ed Bangs, "they readily fed upon."

October 23, 1990. Rifle season had been on for two days, and the pups were still coming back to the rendezvous site each night from farther- and farther-flung rambles, and—this is what quickened the heart—they weren't feeding much on the deer Jimenez left for them.

"They have been observed for several days at one location,"

wrote Bangs, "indicating that they may have made a kill of either a hunter cripple or are feeding on a gut-pile."

This was information that had to be found out by the biologists, if at all possible. After the pups left the location, the biologists moved in to examine the area, but no carcasses were found. It's the greatest thing about studying them, or about just knowing they're out there: their mystery. Maybe they ate all traces of the kill—hide, hooves, bones and all, as they often do—or maybe they were just hanging out, resting, being mysterious.

November. "The pups have grown into full-size adults," Bangs wrote, "and seem to be very wary of humans. Vehicle noises send them scattering to cover and they tend to avoid humans. They have, on several occasions, passed through a pasture containing several head of goats. Although the landowner was concerned, she was not alarmed and made efforts to keep the flock closer to the house. There was no indication that the wolves made any attempt to bother the goats.

"The pack seems to be relying less and less on the deer provided for them. Fresh scats are found containing ungulate hair indicating that the wolves are obtaining deer on their own. Some of these could possibly be hunter cripples."

I love the notion that the hunters have sustained the pups. And many hunters are much in favor of having wolves back in the woods—there's nothing harder to stereotype than "a hunter." But it might not be too much of a leap to say that in many instances, the hunters who cripple their deer are slob hunters who take poor, unsporting shots or who are poor marksmen—bellies heaving perhaps as they labor to aim the rifle, jerking the barrel off target in their fat-tremors so that the shot blows out the deer's stomach, or hind leg.

I like to think of the wolves giving chase, then, and pulling that agony-deer down; and I like to think that those hunters—who are generally not the type who are in favor of wolves, but rather, feel in competition with the wolves—have *sustained* their competitors.

The last deer Jimenez put out at the rendezvous site was on November 19th; the pups didn't touch it.

On December 23, Jimenez found what he was looking for. There was blood in the snow, and the wolves had left a chase trail—there were tracks everywhere, "a minimum of four wolves and quite possibly six," according to Jimenez. The pups had become free and floating, hunting, killing, and they had—perhaps with the aid of all of Jimenez's propped-up and belly-opened road kills—taught themselves to hunt and to kill. The carcass was completely consumed except for the pelvis, scattered bone chips, and a leg.

Suddenly the Ninemile orphans blossomed. They went from being "home boys," as Jimenez called them, into *wolves*—which is to say, travelers. Checking out new territory, going over into adjacent valleys, crossing ridges, but always, returning home.

Sherry Devlin and other *Missoulian* reporters were in the newsroom on the day before Christmas Eve, the day Jimenez found the for-sure kill with the telltale tracks and the takedown from behind. To say that Jimenez was excited would be more than a mild understatement.

"It was really kind of cold, real snowy," Devlin remembers. "We're all standing in the newsroom, and someone looks out the window and says, 'Hey Sherry, here comes Jimenez.' And he's coming in with this *deer leg*," Devlin says. It's dusk, and Jimenez, bloody and muddy and wet and happy, is coming through the falling snow, having come straight in from the field with his proof. "He was just *beaming*," says Devlin.

Jimenez was waving the deer leg all around, rapping on the window with it, and Devlin went outside to meet him.

"He was just beside himself," she says. "He didn't know if he should bring the leg inside the newsroom, so he propped it up against a newspaper box outside.

"All he kept saying, over and over, was, 'They did it just like wolves do it. *They did it just like wolves do it.*' He'd been so afraid he was going to teach them something human," says Devlin.

Ralph Thisted laughs, remembering the day, too. "He came up to our place, waving that same chewed-up leg all around," he says. "I told him, 'Heck, come on in if you're that hungry, we've got some food in the house.'"

"I was like, *wow*," Jimenez says, even now, months later, laughing. "It was like when your kids go off to school for the first time. You know, when they get on the bus by themselves. Yeah, we were tickled. We got caught up with it, too," he says. "It's hard not to. The goal is to recover the population. The problem is that you do it through individuals—and when you deal with 'em on a continuous basis, it's real tough. You try not to get involved.

"It's hard. And a lot of researchers . . ." Jimenez shakes his head. "It's real hard. You know, you're trying to stay objective and do the research, and yet at the same time, there's an attachment that you try and avoid."

"He was as proud of that deer leg as if it were his child's first lost tooth," Devlin says. "All he kept saying was, 'They did it just like wolves do it.'"

SEVEN

Similar to the Montana story of wolves is Mexico's.

A map showing the tiny (suspected) remaining home range of Mexican wolves is almost a mirror image of the gray wolf's shrunken range in the United States' northern Rockies. Because there may be only ten or fifteen wild wolves left in all of Mexico, the USF&WS has hired the legendary Roy McBride to help live-trap Mexican wolves for breeding purposes and genetic preservation—and for possible reintroduction, if a site can ever be found that is both a biological as well as a political fit. To date, none has been discovered. It's the Montana story, only in a different language. Poison—the deadly "1080" has been outlawed in the U.S. though not in Mexico—as well as trapping, mining, logging and overgrazing by both American-owned and Mexican-owned operations all conspire in their usual manner to erase the wolf. The drug operations of the Mexican backwoods are one of the few hopes Mexican wolves have, in that such desperadoes tend to displace the ranchers and loggers.

The Mexican revolution of 1910 released large private ranches to the peasants and the result, Roy McBride writes, was "the conversion of large, thinly settled ranches into rural areas (called *ejidos*) with tremendous human population. The impact of the *ejido* on the wildlife and environment has been devastating. Trees are used for firewood, grass is consumed by herds of burros and horses, and wildlife is used as a food source whenever possible. Conservation is a luxury unheard of in most areas, and the luxury of setting aside areas such as national parks which would preserve large mammals cannot be afforded under the demands of the agrarian system that now exists."

McBride—who helped livestock interests trap the last wolves in Mexico, usually wolves who'd been injured in traps and turned exclusively to cattle, such as the famous Las Margaritas—caught the wolves when no one else could.

Las Margaritas worked cattle in the Mexican state of Durango and sometimes Zacatecas; she was missing two toes from her front left foot, having pulled free of a trap. McBride was trapping for two younger wolves in Durango for the Cattlemen's Union. Around this time Las Margaritas moved in to the ranch McBride was trapping. The tracks of the injured left foot indicated that she was responsible in April for thirteen steers. Las Margaritas went west in May and killed more cattle elsewhere, then in June came back to the ranch where McBride was still working.

David Brown tells the story in his book, *The Wolf in the Southwest*.

"Characteristically, the wolf seldom used the same trail twice. If it came into a pasture by a log road, it left by a cow trail.

"McBride was certain he could catch the wolf if he could get it near a trap. Finally, at the end of July, the wolf came down a washed-out log road and passed one of McBride's trap sets. The wolf smelled the trap, turned back, and trotted up to it, barely missing the trigger with the gap caused by the missing toes. The wolf then apparently suspected the trap and left the road.

"In October McBride found where Las Margaritas had urinated on a small juniper beside a logging road; he carefully placed a set there. Two weeks later the wolf passed by the trap, advanced a few steps towards it, and then ran down the road. The only scent on the bush was its own, and McBride could not understand how the wolf knew the trap was there. Las Margaritas then moved to a new area . . .

"A pair of wolves showed up in this area in November and began killing in the same pasture in which Las Margaritas was operating. Several days after their arrival, McBride picked up fresh tracks that the two wolves had made before the dew. He also saw Las Margaritas's tracks but they were made after the dew had formed. While trailing them, McBride noticed that whenever the male of the pair left the road to make a scent station, Las Margaritas never investigated but continued down the road." Perhaps she remembered McBride's trap for her in that small juniper that had been her own scent station in October.

"Finally, the pair of wolves came to one of McBride's traps, and the female was caught. When Las Margaritas came to where the trap had been pulled out of the ground, the wolf left the road and disappeared until December."

McBride kept setting traps on into January, while Las Margaritas was off killing cattle elsewhere. McBride boiled the traps with oak leaves, and when setting the traps was careful not to step on the ground, instead dismounting from his horse onto a steer hide placed on the ground. McBride buried the traps with dirt run through a sifter to make the surface above the trap indistinguishable from anywhere else.

Finally Las Margaritas came back and passed right over McBride's waiting "blind" traps (unbaited, and still buried), coming within a few feet of each trap but leaving the trail each time she came upon the spots where the traps were buried. McBride later caught a coyote in the set; more education for Las Margaritas. She left again and began killing cattle on a ranch about fifteen miles west.

"By March," Brown writes, "McBride was convinced that he would never catch this wolf."

McBride had noticed that Las Margaritas would sometimes investigate the remains of campfires along the roads where log-truck drivers had stopped to cook. (Brown points out that one of the reasons wolves use trails and roads is that wolves take great care of their feet, keeping them in shape for the chase.) McBride built a fire over a trap and let it burn out, then placed a piece of dried skunk hide next to the ashes.

"On March 15 the wolf came down the road, winded the ashes and skunk hide, and walked over to investigate. Las Margaritas was caught by the crippled foot and the trap held. There was much celebration among the ranchers the following day." Reading this, I'm reminded of the celebration the wolves were able to engender among Jimenez and the newspaper staff. It seems only fair that if we try to control wolves, at least they can control our emotions.

In eleven months of intensive effort and several thousand miles on horseback, McBride had managed to get the wolf near a trap only four times.

"Taking" is the verb McBride uses when he traps animals.

McBride worked for several years for the Animal Damage Control. In his spare time, he earned a degree in wildlife management which, writes Don Schueler in his book, *Incident at Ea-*

gle Ranch, "enables him to combine the 'scientific perspective' and the jargon of the trapper with the knowledge of the trapper in the field."

McBride is such a legend in the Southwest that on both sides of the border a motto developed, "Let McBride do it." "During his younger days," Schueler writes, "he had more to do with bringing the mountain lion to the verge of extinction in Texas than any other single person. Given his remarkable stamina and the quality of his pack of hounds, a lion 'almost never gets away' once McBride goes after it."

"Roy McBride does not like sheep, or more exactly, he does not like what they have done to much of the western range," writes Schueler. "When asked if he considered himself a conservationist, he laughed and said, 'Hell no.' The fact is that he shares with other predator hunters an addiction to the work itself."

I heard McBride speak in a crowded auditorium at the 1990 Arizona Wolf Symposium, in a room with hundreds of people who were lusting to save the same wolves he had killed for so long. McBride had trapped several wolves and had observed Mexican wolves in the wild more closely than anyone in the room and probably knew more about them than anyone present. There was a strange mix of disbelief—not quite anger—and hard jealousy in the air when he got up to speak. How could you be for wolves and *for* someone like McBride? The audience was grudgingly attracted to him.

"I've done it all," McBride says calmly. "I've worked with the reintroduction of the Mexican wolf, and Mexican grizzly." He speaks without a text, holding his big hat in his hands. McBride is lean, flat-bellied, square-jawed, tall and boyish-looking. We can't recognize him as prey, or enemy—he doesn't fit our image.

McBride looks out across at us and continues his modest yet accurate understatements.

"I've done some work in Mexico tracking wolves," he says. "It's kind of sad that there's this many people around interested in them and not any of 'em left around to work with.

"I think I had the best job anybody ever had," McBride says, speaking quietly, and he talks of prowling the oak mountains of the Sierra Madres, the wilderness Mexican states of Durango, Chihuahua, Zacatecas and Sonora. "It was worth it to get to see those tracks and the things they did. I had no idea we could ever get rid of them," he says. "There just wasn't any support to try and preserve them." McBride continues to look out at us. "Or if there was, you didn't know who they were."

What McBride says he remembers most about the work is how *slow* it was—how it took weeks, and then months, to catch a wolf—how you had to wait, and wait. He never had the advantage of snow that trackers in the north have.

"I never had any grudge against them," he says, talking about the wolves. It occurs to me that he's speaking as if they—the Mexican wolves—are goners for sure.

A lot of the wolf experts at the conference want to ask McBride some questions. He's speaking slowly, carefully, as if he's half-somewhere else; half-thinking, but half-remembering.

"Do you think there are any wolves left?" a biologist asks.

"Yeah," McBride says.

"A viable breeding population?"

"No," McBride says.

"Roy, I'd like to ask you a tough question," says the biologist.

"Okay."

"Could you name some places in the United States that would be good places for reintroduction?"

McBride shrugs. "A lot of the national forests would be excellent," he says. "The Coronado National Forest." (The Coronado National Forest carries a high population of cattle.) McBride shrugs again.

"You need an enormous area to support a few wolves, and they would go outside the boundaries exploring, and the young would roam too," McBride says. "All the government agencies are politically run—that's how they get their funding. They must be sensitive to their issues. I think it's difficult to expect them to do that," McBride says—meaning, difficult for the government to bring back the wolf. He's still turning his hat in his hands, and he looks up, not unpleasantly. "Maybe you well-wishers and well-meaners should take on the problem yourselves."

"How do you view Big Bend?" asks another biologist.

"They would be outside that park before you got your truck turned around."

There's a strange stillness in the room—the dullness that bad news brings, bad news from an expert—and McBride, of course, feels it as clearly as anyone. The room's silent for some time, as if it's a wake, and to break his discomfort McBride turns to the person sitting next to him and nudges him and says, "You were standing right there next to a trapper and didn't even know it." We all laugh and do the thing that can so characterize our species; we feel happiness roll right up our arms. McBride knows our species as well as he knows wolves.

Don Schueler writes, in *Incident at Eagle Ranch*, "'Which is neater,' Roy McBride asked me, 'the lion or the deer?'

"The lion, of course. It is the more majestic, less common, more uncompromising of the two animals. Furthermore, in a human scale of values we are obliged to admit that the predator is always neater than its prey if we are to justify our cheerful certainty that we are the neatest thing on earth . . ."

In that balance, Schueler points out, any mountain lion or wolf is worth exactly as many deer as it must kill to stay alive.

"There're going to be problems," McBride says, "and you're going to have to be ready for that. The thing we need to be glad for is they don't eat people."

That was in the spring of 1990. In the fall of 1991 court records concerning a federal raid on an illegal poisons lab in Wyoming included McBride's name, calling him a "pesticide trafficker." The court accused the lab of the "widespread illegal sale" and use of "highly toxic" pesticides that have been used allegedly to kill the usual list of range "pests": bald eagles, golden eagles, coyotes, foxes, skunks, prairie dogs, and any passing-by wolves that try to come into the country, as well as anything else that tries to dislodge the bait in which the poison is hidden. The federal court's affidavit also indicates that the traffickers sold banned poisons (cyanide shells) to the former ADC district director in Oklahoma. (A cyanide shell slides into a cyanide gun, which is buried in the ground beneath the bait and wired with gunpowder so that it blasts into the mouth or face of whatever dislodges the bait.)

I hope McBride is innocent. I remember him lambasting the Japanese government for continuing to sell what he called "dark-of-the-moon 1080" to ranchers in Mexico. And then I think of what it would be like for a man like McBride to be in jail, trapped by iron.

It is all too complex for me, all the stories outside of wolves. It would be so lovely to not have to follow the scents of the politics, the laws, the cattle, the humans, the hunters, the roads. It would be so lovely to just stay in the dark woods and concentrate only on pure unencumbered biology: foot sizes and body weights, diets, range and distribution. It would also be fiction.

Not everyone knows about wolves—about the way they are. Even the biologists are surprised by the way their actions shift and flow, the mark of a creative and responsive intelligence. Some people seem to know less about the facts of wolves than others. For every Mike Jimenez, there seems to be a thousand Troy Maders and John Cargills, and their hopped-up, wild-eyed congressmen such as Ron "No Wolves No Where No Way" Marlenee.

Troy Mader went to college for a year and a half at Grand Canyon University, and then came home to work for what is called the Common Man Institute in Gillette, Wyoming. The Common Man Institute is run by Mader's father, Dick, who calls himself The Freedom Prospector. The family's income is derived mainly from auctioneering and real estate sales.

The theme of the Common Man Institute is that wolves are bad, even demonic, and that the people who support them are no better. "Facts show wolf promoters and wildlife nature-first groups are predator promoters who destroy wildlife," writes Dick Mader, the Freedom Prospector.

John Cargill is a guide, outfitter and taxidermist in Whitehall, Montana, who sent out a letter to rod and gun clubs and fly-fishing clubs across the state, along with one of the Common Man's videos, narrated by and starring an extremely awkward and young-looking Troy Mader.

"Dear Sportsmen," Cargill writes.

"In [*sic*] behalf of the Montana Outfitters and Guides Association we would like to help inform the public of the many problems and facts that come along with the proposed Wold [*sic*]

Reintroduction to Montana, Idaho and Wyoming. The enclosed video is 20 minutes and loaded with facts.

"Only constant public pressure will help to derail this train before it gets too far out of control. The head wind has slowed it down for now thanks to concerned persons but the wolf people will try other avenues in the future, I'm sure to get wolves wherever they can in any state.

"It is a possible way to stop hunting, no game, shorter seasons and possible [*sic*] no hunting at all in certain areas. Recreational accesses will be curtailed to allow for potential denning sights [*sic*] where wolves are allowed. All sportsmen, residents and non-residents alike want to keep their hunting opportunities that we have fought for and pay for. Share the information with whom you can to let everyone know that the wolf is a meat eating machine and will be devastating to the wildlife we have as well as livestock and domestic animals.

" 'SAY NO TO WOLVES'

"Any donations your club can contribute would be appreciated to help MOGA cover costs. For further information contact me anytime.

"John C. Cargill"

In the video, Mader stands in front of the camera in a navy blazer looking glassy-eyed, reminding me of a vampire. He rocks slightly from foot to foot like a small boy who has to go to the bathroom as he explains what wolves will do to this country.

"The U.S. has a history of conservation," Mader says, "and India, for example, has a history of environmentalism, and in India, wolves eat children."

Moving quickly, as if to escape judgment from the truth, Mader leaps from this stunningly inaccurate logic to show slides of a few old bloated cows and several heinie shots of torn-out horses' asses and chewed-up hamstrings, horses whose owners did not protect them. Mader then tells the story—his young voice breaking—of an island in Alaska where, now that wolves have been trapped off that island and kept off, "huntin' season is six months long, and hunters' bag limit is six deer per hunter." (Just what every hunter needs—a good half-ton of venison, one or two tons per family.)

Then Mader dispels the notion that wolves exert a selective influence on game populations—that they do not, as biologists state, prey on the slower, weaker animals. Mader does this by showing a photograph of an old cow moose.

They didn't get this one—yet. "How come?" he wants to know.

Mader switches tack abruptly.

"We can go Man's way, or nature's way," he says, and then shows us slides of bad old nature's way, with each atrocity labeled in bold letters: *Fire* (a picture of Yellowstone)—*Starvation* (a picture of some unidentifiable bones)—*Predation* (more bones).

Mader doesn't mention what Man's glorious way is.

Then it's back to the photographs, the still shots, of dead horses. One in particular seems to horrify Mader. "So much of the rectal cavity was eaten that she couldn't *function*," Mader says, with what sounds like almost a strange fascination. And then a picture of a dead deer, which is what wolves eat. "This deer was eaten alive, the game warden told me," Mader testifies. "'How could you tell?' I asked. The conservation officer said the deer's eyes were open."

Mader tells us that wolves will mean closing Yellowstone to the public, and then his voice grows hypnotic, dreamy, even ghoulish.

"I'd like to show you what you'll see if wolves are brought

back," Mader says, and shows pictures of skeletons and bones—not mass Jonestown piles of them, but just a bleached leg bone here, a well-gleaned rib cage or skull there . . . The implication is, of course, that if wolves are *not* brought back, we'll never die, not under Man's way, and we'll all be lifted up glorious and whole, with our rectums still functioning, never to have anything to do with that messy boneyard . . .

"Wolves even kill wolves," Mader says, and then, with a sneer, "You may even be fortunate enough to look out the kitchen window and watch five wolves kill one buck deer. Thank you, ladies and gentlemen."

EIGHT

It wasn't enough that the Ninemile wolves had beaten the odds and survived, and had shunned livestock. It wasn't enough to startle; they had to amaze.

On January 22nd, 1991, Jimenez found the remains of another deer that the wolves had caught, killed, and eaten—a yearling spike buck—and with it, he found raw new science, mysticism, and confusion.

There was a paired urine scent mark at the kill site, which indicated pair-bonding—one of the preliminary phases of mating—and stranger yet, Jimenez found blood in one of the scent marks, indicating a female in estrus. Wolves typically begin bonding, courting, in the late fall, and breed in late January, or sometimes even as late as the end of February. Sixty-three days later (the same as dogs), the pups are born, weighing about a pound each.

Blood in the urine of one of the Ninemile orphans was almost unthinkable. Wolves in a pack don't even begin to consider mating until their second year, and usually not before their third year. Physically mature at the age of five or six months, within the community of the pack they typically come into "emotional" maturity in their second summer of life, when they're fourteen months old. Sometimes they disperse at that point, splitting off from the pack if they have notions of grandeur, ideas of becoming alphas somewhere else.

And then they breed, if they find and win a mate, that next January or February, at the age of roughly twenty-two months. But that's the earliest known timetable, and wolves who do breed that early, says David Mech, usually do so only in captivity, perhaps due to the lack of a complex social structure. Early-breeding wolves usually have only one or two pups, unlike dogs, who have normal-sized litters even if bred in the first year of life.

There's not much known about the relationship between wolf sociology and wolf behavior, and its effect on their biology. It's been theorized that, for example, the alpha female, once she's won that position, will dominate the other females in the pack with such ferocity that the other females are psychologically or physiologically inhibited from entering estrus. Down in Mexico, a captive alpha female Mexican wolf killed the beta female, a crushing loss to that species' tiny remaining gene pool.

Perhaps the opposite was true here: perhaps the hardships of their existence caused an early behavioral maturity. "They're real mature," Jimenez said.

From the very beginning, the biologists had been noticing that when they howled to see if the pups would answer, there was one howl that came back deeper when the pups were at the rendezvous site, feeding on game. It could have been an older wolf who'd joined them—extremely unlikely, as no such wolf was ever seen with the pups—or it could have been that, even then, one of the pups was feeling more confident: king of the mountain, on top of that carcass, and already dominating, already assuming the pack's leadership positions with no adults around to back him down. The alpha.

Jimenez kept finding those pair-bonded urine marks—the blood-urine of the female down low, with the leg-lifted scent of the male right above it. But still, after further research, the general belief was that the wolves hadn't mated—or that if they had, no pregnancy had resulted. Ralph Thisted had seen two of the wolves attempting to breed at the far edge of the pasture—or what *looked* like attempts to breed—but he couldn't tell if it was the male and female with the collars who were trying to mate, or not.

"She did come into heat," Jimenez stated emphatically, in March. "It'd be real neat. It'd be real unusual," he said, speaking of a possible pregnancy. Jimenez thought for a moment and then said, "It'd almost be *typical* for these guys, since they've done everything we didn't think they'd do so far anyway. But it would be a real slim chance that she is pregnant."

I worried at the time about relocating a pregnant, or possibly pregnant female—about the effects the tranquilizing drugs might have on her, if there was livestock depredation and she had to be relocated. And about home, and denning, and about whether she'd take one last road trip, one last fling before giving birth. If she was pregnant.

Joe Fontaine answered that question glumly. "The state has still requested that if we do any relocations, we do them in Glacier National Park. Anything that they're managing for ungulate populations basically is off-limits."

Jimenez laughed; and he could maybe afford to laugh, because it was March, and he had four wolves, maybe six, in this valley, with reports of another adult a valley or two away. And maybe one of his pups was pregnant, and they were killing deer, hunting fine, and ignoring cows and calves—in March, there were baby calves being dropped all *over* the valley—and baby chickens and ducks and geese and goats.

"Thanks but no thanks," Jimenez laughed, speaking for the state: the state that professes a desire to manage the wolves.

The net.

The wolves moving beneath it.

"What about the big private places, like Ted Turner's ranch, and guys like that?" I asked.

Fontaine answered. "We haven't really approached 'em. There's all kinds of possibilities," he said.

Hard releases versus soft releases. And . . .

Thank God the politicians' bellies are too large to allow them to get into the woods. Thank goodness the flat-bottomed soles of their shoes are too slippery to allow them to scramble up the rock cliffs and to move into and through the trees, chasing the wolves *physically*. Thank goodness the wolves can run faster.

The best the politicians can do is *react*—they can't control. They can legislate, and pout, and cast a great throw-net over the northwestern part of the state, but there are wolves moving through the woods, and in some places the net gets hung up in the trees and the wolves keep going, traveling, living wild lives, increasing a sphere which is nearing Yellowstone. It's a perfect example of how wilderness areas and national parks, in the old days, were created without the increasingly important concept of "migration corridors" in mind—but that's another story, and we need to swing back, as ever, to the orphans, to the Ninemile, and see if there was indeed a pregnant female . . .

Ralph and Bruce saw the pups "attempting" to breed again, and this time saw that it *was* the collared pair.

In a pack of two males and two females, there's not enough variation for a scientist to make any kind of guesses whatsoever—chance, not predictability, must always be suspect—but a writer has no such constraints, and I believe the old rumor I've heard that for better or worse a radio collar can sometimes actually improve a wolf's social standing as well as survivability. One certain advantage to the population, if not the individual, says biologist Mike Fairchild, is that radio telemetry "allows the wolf to tell us what it likes—what's good wolf habitat—rather than our trying to guess."

Other proponents of radio collars say that it's possible that the collars help by providing protection to the wolf's neck during battles with alien wolves, or even within the pack, which would in turn almost *assure* dominance (which would then be a human-inspired foul-up, a selection of weak, trappable wolves, because collared wolves are the ones who weren't clever or wild enough or experienced enough to avoid the trap in the first place).

It's also been theorized, however, that, ethics and wild morality aside, the collar (sometimes a 4 percent to 7 percent increase relative to body weight) can stress the animal into the zone of increased mortality. The collar can get caught on branches, can make the animal more visible to predators, including man, and may require too many extra calories to carry around, too much weight to run down game effectively.

I'm not much on radio collars, though it doesn't really matter what my thoughts are. I understand that they can be used, like anything, with discretion or without discretion. The wolves I've seen in the wild have not had radio collars, and I'm glad for it.

I've seen grizzly bears with and without radio collars and seeing a grizzly with a collar does nothing for me; seeing one *without* does everything. Just behind the collar are trappers, helicopters, computers—*knowledge*, instead of mystery.

We could talk for a long while about radio collars—about how the wolf-pack members groom each other and try to chew them off their leaders' necks; about how even the longest-lasting batteries are only good for two to three years, and then you've got to retrap the wolves (good luck, on your second attempt). But the story I like best involves not wolves, but rather, birds—some wild-ass colored little songbird, down in the Amazon I think, is how the story goes. And it may not even have been a radio transmitter they banded to this little songbird's leg—call it a bright blue and yellow bird; it may have just been a red band, with a number.

The band brightly colored, so it could be seen easily, even when the bird was flying through the trees.

The researchers spent their springtime crouching in the ferns, watching "their" birds court and spoon: the birds hopping up and down on boulders, singing, trilling, preening and strutting, displaying their bright feathers—and all the females *ignored* these banded males.

It turned out that the birds had evolved a specific, genetic courtship response to those specific colors—blue and yellow, in the right combination—and now there was this *red* shit all around the males' legs.

There was no reproduction that year, among this group of the species, and the researchers sat back in the ferns and turned to one another and said, "Wha'? Wha'd we do?"

One more example of how wolf technocracy can run amok, can pierce some people's sensibilities (mine included) regarding the manners in which a wild animal with an intricate social structure can be studied with morals kept intact, follows:

Biologists are experimenting with an ultraviolet dye. They mix different quantities, different concentrations of it and label the jars of the u-v fluid based on *isotope* numbers, or some damn thing. When they catch a wolf they shoot the wolf full of this xenophobic glowing *fluid*—call it XL-121, for the black female, and XL-128, for the gray male pup; give the old male, say, a shot of XL-135—and then when the biologists come upon wolf shit in the woods, they can wave this *wand* over it—this battery-powered hand-held black light—and they can tell by the way it glows what particular wolf shat that shit.

I'm not sure what my logic tells me about this—the pluses and minuses. I know how I *feel* about it: I don't like it and want to keep it to a bare minimum. But sometimes special steps are necessary to give the wolves, even one or two of them, even the remotest bit of a break, and breathing space.

It's not the wolves who are captured and collared or injected with xeno-dye who get the break, however. Those are the ones who sacrifice, who give the break, by being studied, to the ones who aren't studied.

The wild ones slip away, back and deeper into the woods, wilder than ever, now. They need to receive that luck.

NINE

It was time—March, 1991—for me to go into the woods and see where these four pups were hanging out. Despite USF&WS's disclaimers and qualifications about the blood-in-urine and paired-scent markings, I felt sure the little black collared female was pregnant. Cows in the Ninemile Valley were dropping calves like crazy. Golden eagles sat in the high cottonwoods along the river, waiting to swoop down on the afterbirth once the cow had moved the calf off to safety. There were also baby ducks, baby goats, and baby geese all through the valley. "It's like a *nursery* out there," Ed Bangs said.

The snow would be gone in a month, rendering, one hoped, the wolves invisible again.

Although Jimenez and Joe Fontaine had been dodging such media requests all winter—"Take me out to see where the wolves live"—they capitulated; I got to ride along in the police car, so to speak. We drank our coffee—about three gallons' worth—

and talked about wolves. Wolf biologists love to talk about wolves—but going out into the field with other humans is not high on their list of wants. You start talking that way, making requests on their woods time, their wilderness time, and they disappear. They protect their privacy, and I understand that. It's as if the woods are the only place where they can go to be alone.

The biologists understand and respect the wolves' extreme wariness. It's a rare experience for the biologists to even see a wolf—mostly they just follow closely behind, a day, two days back, in the snow—and they move in the opposite direction, out of respect.

David Mech, who's the hardest of wolf biologists to get in touch with, has a whole *pack* of subordinate student and assistant researchers who screen his calls. It's easier to get through on a line to the White House than to Mech. You can picture him standing there watching one of his research assistants glance at him and say into the telephone, "Ah, he's not here right now, but if you'll leave your name and number and what this is in *reference* to, we can give him the message . . ."

Diane Boyd, the wolf researcher up in Polebridge, Montana, is much the same way. I sent some earnest questions up to her, asking specifically about her studies of wolf–coyote dynamics on the North Fork of the Flathead, and she responded generously, immediately, providing not only the studies I'd requested but phone numbers where she could be reached over Thanksgiving, down in Missoula. There's no telephone service at her cabin in Polebridge.

But early into our correspondence, I made the mistake of leaving my *scent*—the scent of my desire, my wish to go into the woods with her, into her wolves' woods—and she vanished, and I have not been able to get back in touch with her since making that request, have not been able to find her.

They're busy, and they're private. Mech finally and generously acquiesced to have one of his assistants fly me over Isle Royale in northern Michigan, where he works—but then *I* ran out of time, and the trip fell through. Renée Askins, my friend down in Moose, head of the Wolf Fund, volunteered bravely to let me go up with *her* into British Columbia with her friend, Lu Carbyn, head of Canada's wildlife department, to look at Canada's wolves. These wolves would possibly be the stock, the source, for a Yellowstone reintroduction, if the wolves don't first repopulate it themselves, but that trip, too, fell through. I like to picture Lu Carbyn shouting, "You volunteered *what*? And somebody I don't even know?"

We're in the big Ford pickup, Mike's personal truck, bouncing down the Ninemile road. Whitetails, out in the middle of the day, bound right in front of the truck, barely missing the front bumper. They leap acrobatically over the barbed-wire fences and canter out into the center of the ranchers' stubbly cow-mowed feedlots. They stop and turn their graceful necks and look back at us as if *desiring* to be chased. Other deer are leaping in and out of the horses' corrals, and deer are running down the road in front of us as we head north up the skinny valley, with the truck's four-wheel drive spinning in more than half a foot of new wet snow.

There are little Hereford calves lying down in the snow everywhere, just as Bangs had said, being licked and cleaned by their mothers. There are dozens of little red furry mounds in the snow, their steaming warmth having cleared a small patch of bare earth in the white stretch of field. Some black Angus stand stocky-legged at the far end of the pasture, with the new white spring snow, and brilliant red budding willows flame along the river's run. Ravens and eagles sit in the trees and watch, and wait.

Every one of these cows, and their calves, is living so that it may be eaten by something or someone; all eyes covet it, I think, and the mothers continue to lick their calves dry, with more steam rising.

"Those types of things key predators," Jimenez says. "Eagles coming in to the afterbirth, and blood on the snow . . ." It makes predators realize there's new meat in town, is what he's saying, and it seems a miracle the wolves haven't come down in the night, or even in the dusky stormy daytime, and raided the fields.

I think everything's okay.

We're surrounded by mountains. The tiny valley's as flat as a pancake, but all around us there are immense, romantic mountains; and all of these mountains, in all directions, have rumors of wolves.

Mike points behind us, to the steep, snowy faces that are taller than all of the others—Zeus- and Olympus-looking mountains.

"Cat hunters," he says (mountain lion hunters, who take snowmobiles and dogs far into the mountains, in the dead of winter), "pick up wolf tracks on the other side of the interstate." Those are old, long-disregarded rumors—that there are wolves way up there, to the south: in the Fish Creek drainage.

Maybe they're not rumors. Maybe not this year, anyway.

The mountains that lie across the interstate from the Ninemile Valley are the ones that intrigue me the most. No one lives there, in the Fish Creek area. They're incredibly rugged-looking. They join up with the knife ridge of the Bitterroots, which tightropes the Montana–Idaho line before depositing wild creatures, a couple hundred miles later, into the West Yellowstone area.

We should have some kind of confetti ready for when the first wolf slips into Yellowstone. We should have field mice and rabbits ready, and should line both sides of the street and be ready, waiting, when he or she comes trotting in, as if finishing—or beginning—the longest of marathons. We could shower the wolf with the mice and rabbits as if throwing rice at a wedding.

"I see you, Mister Wolf," Irene Newman kept saying, standing on her back porch and peering out into the gloom of her orchard, with the wolf watching her back, as well.

As long as they don't figure out those cows are prey, it'll be okay, I think. One of the old wives' tales that's enshrined in the ranching as well as environmental community is that wolves prefer wild meat to beef—that beef tastes rancid to the wolves. That tale has been around so long that it quite possibly, as with several old wives' tales, has as-yet-undiscovered scientific validity to it— but it doesn't really matter, I suppose, to either the rancher or the cows whether the wolf simply enjoys or *relishes* the meat. Once it's done, it's done, and there seems to be little comfort to be gotten from the idea that "Oh well, the wolf probably didn't enjoy it that much."

We turn up a canyon where Mike saw tracks in the snow the week before. The new snow will tell a better tale of immediacy and direction and habits—*function*—than the rather cumbersome H-bar antennae that simply beeps and tells you (sometimes) that the wolves are still out there (the collared wolves, anyway) and in what approximate direction they're located. In steep forested and rocky canyons such as the mountains surrounding the Ninemile, and in much of northwestern Montana and northern

Idaho, the collar signals can't be picked up from the ground, and the dreaded overflights—surveillance by aircraft—are necessary to pick up signals that, down on the ground, bounce around the canyons and give ricocheting, muted readings, utter electronic gibberish.

I'm glad that we're on the ground. It's bad enough to have the electronic box in our hands, but from a plane, it would seem much, much worse. In his book, *Grizzly Years*, Doug Peacock writes beautifully and with comprehensive finality about his own loathing of aircraft surveillance of wild animals—of aircraft in general, in fact, and their relation to the wilderness.

"The next morning I was gliding across the frozen snow in the middle of a mile-wide meadow when I heard the droning of an airplane engine. Instinctively, I raced for a small clump of sagebrush, kicked off my snowshoes, threw down the pack, and covered everything up with a white sheet I had at the top of my pack, hoping my tracks would not be visible from a thousand feet up. I never feel so naked or vulnerable as when I am hiding in the open from aircraft . . .

"The small plane passed . . . There ought to be a few places out of which we keep aircraft, or keep them high enough so as not to be intrusive. What is the point of designating a two-dimensional wilderness and permitting the buzzing or hovering of a helicopter at tree level? This place, so wild and big this time of year on foot, can be shrunk to a small, tame landscape by machines."

TEN

We're sliding in the truck, up into ever deeper snow, up a canyon and past a few almost hidden boarded-up-for-winter homes, and then into national forest. After a while Mike stops the truck, and he and Joe get out and examine one set of enormous tracks, and Mike says, with some puzzlement and perhaps a little worry, "They're back."

Jimenez doesn't like it when the wolves are too predictable—when they hang out in one area too much, and too regularly. He wants them to be *wolves*, to travel. They were in this one canyon almost all of last week, and he hadn't been able to find a kill that would have explained their temporary encampment in this one forest, and so there's some kind of puzzle piece missing, some roughness.

The snow's deep and the air's cold—around twenty degrees, and wet. A train's faint moan reaches us from the next valley, and I wonder what the wolves think of that—if they ever call back to it. Is it outlandish to think maybe that's one of the things that drew them to this valley—that they were lonely, and liked its sound?

I'm thinking like a poet. I'm thinking foolishly, stupidly. Steve Fritts and Ed Bangs would be distraught to hear me voice such a thought. Joe Fontaine would be annoyed, and would shake his head. Jimenez, I think, would look off in the direction of the faraway moan, and shrug.

It's a good sound. The wind carries it a long, long way.

"There was a raven around here for a while," he says. Things would make more sense to Jimenez if there were a kill. He's a little nervous because Shirley, one of the Ninemile ranchers (it was her dog, Bear, that got "popped" by the big gray male) has a downed cow who can't get up. The cow's been down for over a week now, after giving birth—probably a prolapsed uterus— and she would be easy, attractive prey for the wolves. She's down by the river.

"Shirley's had hard enough luck," Jimenez says. "We're trying to go out of our way to help her." He's looking around for ravens, which could signal a kill, and he's looking at the mountains— looking over toward Alberton, the direction where the wolves have headed once or twice before turning back—and I think Jimenez is thinking like a wolf at that moment: that he's trying to get a handle on things. He's not *theorizing*, but just watching, and waiting.

Which, as I understand it, is exactly how a wolf hunts.

"It would be nice," Jimenez had said, earlier that morning, when I asked him if he thought the wolves would expand their range—*really* expand it.

"There's a lot of uninhabited land pretty close by," he said, "and yeah, I think everybody would be delighted if they'd go a ridge or two over, and hang out there—and live happily ever after. But it's asking a lot of a first-year wolf to pick up and set up a new territory on its own."

We get back in the truck and drive a little farther up the road, axle-deep in the snow. We pass a piece of litter, a plastic trash bag, and Mike stiffens and says that that wasn't here before.

There are wolf tracks—a lot of tracks now—and we get out and follow them a short distance into some willows next to a spring, where we find all manners of bones: deer, mostly. There's wolf scat everywhere.

Someone's done precisely what the biologists have feared—they've been dumping meat. And the wolves have found and eaten it.

Mike and Joe collect the wolves' scat in little plastic bags for analysis.

We find a big bone—a huge bone, a leg bone of some kind, orangey yellow, rancid—as thick around as the neck of a baseball bat. Mike sniffs the joint where a butcher's saw has cut it. There's hay matted to the bone, and it has the tallowy smell of beef.

Mike's concerned—it appears that someone's dumped their old venison, and maybe some old cow or bull parts they'd slaughtered—but he doesn't panic, doesn't say much; the wolves are still out there, still free. It could be the start of something big, though, something very bad.

This is definitely a pro-wolf story. But it's not to say that wolves can't kill the hell out of cattle, if their hearts get turned in that direction. There are perhaps half a hundred stories in the West of renegade wolves who keyed in on *only* cattle—wolves with names not like Puppy or Papa Wolf or the Ninemile Mother, but rather the Black Devil and Bigfoot, the Terror of Lane County.

Stanley Young, the old government wolf-getter with more than a whiff of hyperbole and western myth-longing about him, wrote in his book, *The Last of the Loners*, of a wolf called the Traveler, who without question did immense damage in Arkansas in the 1800s.

"The Traveler . . . would make a kill, eat its fill and then travel forty or fifty miles, never to return to the particular kill."

A wolf like that would be pretty tough to trap—even tough to poison—though eventually, of course, the Traveler was caught.

Old Lefty of Burns Hole, in Eagle County, Colorado, was trapped by the left foot in 1913 and, writes Young, "succeeded in twisting off the better part of his left foot from the trap . . . and then making its escape. As a result of its missing front foot, the stub of which completely healed in time, it had adopted a very peculiar gait. It never put the stub of its left leg to the ground . . . In eight years . . . Old Lefty was credited with the killing of 384 head of livestock."

In reading a history of the famous wolves of the West—the livestock killers, not so strangely, being awarded fame while tales of the Good Mothers such as the Ninemile mom fall away—a picture emerges which does not grant the wolf total absolution from its so-called sin, but which has rarely been commented upon: the preponderance of injuries (combined with a preponderance of cattle) one sees the livestock killers, the "famous" wolves, limping around with.

The Syca Wolf of southern Oregon was an old male with greatly worn teeth, and was credited with killing many horses and cattle. Three Toes of Harding County, South Dakota, had $50,000 worth of killings attributed to him. The Queen Wolf, also called the Unaweep Wolf, wreaked significant havoc in the early twenties, and had a malformed foot caused by a trap injury (she's now on display for eternity at the Colorado Museum of Natural History, her insides stuffed with styrofoam).

The Ghost Wolf of the Judith Basin killed $35,000 worth of livestock in Montana in the twenties and thirties, and seemed to have turned pathologic, often just wounding livestock. The Ghost Wolf had been shot in the hind leg and knocked down, but escaped capture by hiding in a snowdrift where it couldn't be seen. Ranchers tried to run it down in their cars. Once, five Russian wolfhounds cornered and attacked it, battling for hours, but it got away when, writes Bert Lindler, "the wolf escaped up a steep mountainside, with the man, horse and dogs too tired to follow."

Sixty-five traps and poison baits were set out for the Ghost Wolf at a time. Sheep were his rage; at one point, local ranchers had to dispose of forty-three sheep. "Twenty he had killed," said Gus Loberg, now seventy-seven. "The rest he tore up so bad we had to kill 'em."

Bert Lindler interviewed Ed Kolar about his memories of the Ghost Wolf.

"[Kolar] remembers when the wolf killed a short yearling," Lindler wrote in the *Great Falls Tribune* in 1990. " 'The cow came home with the whole rear end torn out of her,' Kolar said. 'We had to kill her.' " The Ghost Wolf was also called the White Wolf. Trappers stayed in the area for five and six months at a time, laying out poison balls and baits, killing everything *but* the White Wolf.

"On May 8, 1930," Lindler writes (with the Ghost Wolf getting up there in years), "Earl Neill and Al E. Close tracked the Ghost Wolf from Close's ranch into Pig Eye Basin in the Little Belt Mountains. They were aided by a German shepherd and an Irish terrier they had trained that winter hunting coyotes.

"The dogs jumped the Ghost Wolf, who fought them. They kept pushing the wolf toward Close, who was hiding behind a tree. When the wolf was forty yards away, Close stepped out.

"'And do you know, I almost didn't shoot,' Close said. 'It was the hardest thing I think I did. There was a perfect shot, the grandest old devil . . . I thought swiftly that these were the hills over which he had hunted. I knew that it was the cruel nature of the wilderness—the fight for the survival of the fittest—that made him the ferocious hunter that he was.

"'Luckily I came to my senses in time and let the bullet fly fairly into the face of the old criminal.'"

In his book *Wildlife in America*, Peter Matthiessen tells of the Custer Wolf killing over $25,000 worth of stock along the Wyoming–South Dakota border in a ten-year reign. "It persistently outwitted the best hunters in the country," Matthiessen writes, "and was said to be accompanied by a parasitic pair of coyotes which, flanking it on both sides, allegedly served as sentinels."

Only after the coyotes were shot was the Custer Wolf killed in October 1920, after another grueling six months of tracking and trap-setting over an area covering 2,600 square miles.

Crip, a clubfooted survivor from a trap in Texas—a red wolf—would sneak in and eat calves at night. Stanley Young reports, "On one ranch alone the animal's telltale tracks were found around seven dead and partly eaten calves . . . As with most of the greatest individual livestock-killing wolves, this animal, although crippled, was nevertheless but little hindered in obtaining food."

It's not a fact that's spoken of enough—or not a hypothesis which has been tested enough, that when wolves go "bad," maybe it's not the whole pack which should be relocated—maybe just the old guy with the worn teeth, the clubfoot . . .

And these aren't the old days: it's impossible for a modern wolf to do such damage. We've got management "tools" we didn't have back at the turn of the century: helicopters, machine guns, even nuclear armaments . . . The fear surrounding wolves and their abilities is so much larger than the animal itself that perhaps our excessive fear *gives* wolves a special, extra power. The wildlife biologists keep trying to educate the West about the truth of wolves, not the myth, but in the meantime, the wolves just keep getting shot.

Jimenez is worried to see his pups eating dumped food for two reasons: it makes them susceptible to being poisoned, and it opens the avenue for their tasting beef and understanding that it is not taboo. Especially for these wolves, who have already made that jump once, the leap from eating dumped food to *hunting* that dumped food.

Neither Joe nor Mike have much to say. They just walk around, picking up pieces of trash and scat and bone. Later Mike will tell me that he thinks the big leg bone we found with the barn hay matted to it was probably not cow, but elk—but I'm not convinced, and I half-wonder if he's saying it to convince himself.

Already this year, Jimenez says, somebody has thrown out the carcass of a deer they had cleaned. "There was a little meat on the bones," he says, "and they found that. It'd be nice if they'd stay away from that kind of stuff," he says. And the month before—February of 1991—a similar catastrophe had been averted.

Twice, Jimenez had had to pick up dead cows in the Ninemile—going out around midnight to get the first one and winching the malodorous carcass out of a ditch and carrying it to the rendering plant in town. The wolves had been in the areas where the cows were dumped, Jimenez says, but hadn't touched either animal.

The secretary-treasurer of the Ninemile Livestock Association, Bob Demins, wrote a letter after that, asking other ranchers in the Ninemile not to dump their cattle anymore, but to instead bury them deep or take them to the rendering plant.

Jimenez looks across a wooded ravine, up to a steep ridge which the winter sun just now, mid-day, is cresting. I think he's *willing* the wolves to get away, to leave this dumping place. It strikes me that that's one of the possible small advantages of having collars on the wolves, when their numbers are so low. Their fates can be known, and would-be poachers will understand that the wolves' movements are being monitored, giving the poachers the feeling, hopefully, that the woods are not as invisible as they once were. (Though that has not stopped poachers from killing radio-collared wolves in the past, almost with abandon. In Minnesota, where there are roughly 1200 wolves, all in the northern half of the state, about twenty-five "problem" wolves are killed each year by federal agents, but poachers, poisoners, kill about two hundred wolves per year.)

It's a strange psychology, a strange pattern, this shooting of radio-collared wolves. I know of at least three instances where biologists or fishermen have found the collar flung into a creek or river, perhaps to drown the telltale, giveaway electronic signal. It's as if the poachers can't just shoot the wolf and then walk away. They have to go *claim* it. Do they cut the collar off to make the wolf be wilder—*not a pet*—and therefore give their feat more validity, more status? But then that act raises the problem of what to *do* with that collar—holding it like a hot potato, perhaps, with a $100,000 fine and a year of jail thundering down.

I like to think that after death, the wolves' souls keep running, faster than ever, that they rise just to the tops of the trees, where they can get a better view. They glance back down at the person who has killed their life-body but nothing can hold them back, they're off and running again, still traveling, flowing, like the northern lights.

"When you try and follow them day to day, it's just mind-boggling," Jimenez says. "You get a fresh snow that erases everything. You're going all over the place, trying to find their tracks, and you find 'em and lose 'em—and then five miles down in another canyon you pick them up again.

"I mean, it's just—they like to *move*. They get this lope—kind of a jog. They have incredible endurance. They'll go over a canyon just to screw around. It's absolutely mind-boggling."

We walk up the road, following the tracks, and Jimenez keeps looking over at the canyon wall. He and Joe take out the portable H-antenna and battery pack, hook it up, and hold it over their heads to try and get some kind of reading. They step up on top of the truck to catch the signals coming in over the tops of the trees, and sure enough, the wolves have gone over the wall again, out of this canyon and into the next. Mike and Joe decide it's safe enough to backtrack, that we won't run much risk of bumping into the wolves and conditioning them to our presence, maybe even allowing ourselves to be associated with the free meal they've just found.

There are snowshoes and cross-country skis in the back of the truck, and even an old snowmobile, but it's so cold that the snow's frozen hard and we can walk across it in our boots alone without punching through.

"In deep snow the wolves tend to do better than the deer," Jimenez says as we enter the woods, following the main course of the huge tracks. What we're looking for is not the wolves themselves, but a kill—to see what they're eating besides the dumped meat, if anything, and how they caught it—and to see why they've been in this one canyon so long. We're a good ten or fifteen miles away from their summer encampment, the site of their youth.

We follow the tracks through the heavy timber, watching and listening for ravens. One lone set of tracks drops into a ravine, and Joe breaks off to follow that set. Mike and I stay up with the rest, and we move through the trees, trying to follow the tracks the way a thread follows a needle, trying to weave up the knowledge of the past two days—what went on, who did what, *everything*. The woods are gloomy and the sky, which we can barely see through the tops of the forest, is promising more snow. Mike moves slowly from track to track with his head bent, sorting, assimilating, trying to count and sort, I think, and I notice that he's careful to never step in one of the tracks.

There are so many of them that it seems we don't have to be so careful, so sparing in our attempts to preserve them—wolf tracks everywhere, and all seeming to go in the same direction, wandering around trees and beneath logs, but moving in a general direction, above and parallel to the creek drainage that Joe disappeared into. But then I realize that it's some *procedure* that's ingrained into Mike, that not stepping on tracks is simply the right way to do the job. He seems lost to this world.

I'm noticing the whole woods, looking all around, comparing them to the woods where I live, and I keep commenting to Mike about all the bright antler-rubbed elk and deer rubs on trees, from where they'd scratched their autumn antlers the previous year. There are big rubs everywhere; big deer and elk leaving them.

Mike looks up from time to time, as if startled, whenever I comment on something above ground level, and he looks at the impressive rubs for a few seconds before turning his attention back to the tracks.

"I had someone in the woods who noticed birds," Mike says pleasantly, following those tracks. "It's interesting what different people key in on."

A little later he stops and looks around. We've come into a deer yard, a place where they've herded together for warmth (and perhaps protection) on the mid-slope, the spot where, each night, warmer air gets sandwiched between rising and falling currents. Mike's looking around at the snow, at the *absence* of wolves, their invisibility, with wonder.

"I was wondering what it must be like to smell that good," he says. There are deer tracks everywhere—the snow in the forest is stippled with them. "It must drive them crazy, having to do all that choosing."

Mike's looking around the woods, just sort of getting *settled* in them, and there's little doubt in my mind that he's wishing he

could scent the way the wolves do; that he even imagines, perhaps, that he's only one step away from being able to.

"You can recreate it," Jimenez says, talking about what it's like
to come upon a kill, in the winter. "Branches get broken, there's
bits of hair and blood . . . " (When we walked up to the trash
bag the wolves had been scavenging, both Joe and Mike had dis-
played an edginess, an extreme caution that had puzzled me at
first until I heard Mike calling, loudly, "Bear? Here, bear!
Bear?"—to make sure no just-out-of-hibernation grizzlies—the
young males coming out first—had also discovered the carcass
and laid claim to it . . .)

Up on the small rocky ridge above us, several large deer are
watching us, and when we turn our attention to them they do
not run, but just stand there, looking back at us.

They should run, I think. We *could* be wolves. How do they
know we won't get them? Is this the "deathwatch" that Lopez
wrote about? Is some sort of communication going on between
us, one which we're not even aware of? Are we saying things to
the deer as we watch them that we don't know we're saying? Are
we out of control?

It's an eerie concept. The deer refuse to run, refuse to be frightened of us.

"I wonder if the deer have it figured out yet," Mike says. "That
predator image—the realization that these wolves are hunting
them. This ecosystem has gone a long time without wolves."

They've gotten used to running from the smaller, less aggressive, less efficient coyotes, and now these *behemoths* are in the
forest, have appeared suddenly in this forest of deer. I like the
idea, and it's one that I've not heard before. Scientists talk at
length about the predator's search image, but what about the

prey's "predator image," and its "escape image"? How does a deer learn to react to being chased by a wolf instead of a coyote? Are different escape strategies used? Do the deer position themselves differently as a herd? Do they realize yet that these wolves are *hunting* them, searching for them—one wolf moving along a creek bottom, perhaps, to flush the deer into flight up along the ridge where the three trailing (perhaps larger, healthier, faster) wolves can then launch the chase?

The deer continue to stand on the bluff a short distance away, just staring at us, looking a little stunned. I've seen deer in the wild for twenty-five years, but I've never had a herd look at me in quite that manner—the manner of none of them, not a one, knowing how to react, *stunned.*

These could be the glory days for the Ninemile, I think; like Yellowstone, it is a valley perfectly suited to the wolves' survival. A whole overpopulated forest of fresh, easy meat, meat which really doesn't even know yet to run. Of course the pendulum will swing, and a balance will be achieved, or will be sought. My Yellowstone friend, Renée Askins, is most fond of the Robinson Jeffers poem:

> *What but the wolf's tooth whittled so fine*
> *The fleet limbs of the antelope?*

We're moving through the shadowy woods. There are deer tracks, wolf tracks everywhere. No signs of the chase, not yet. Just hunting.

"Sometimes the coyotes will follow right behind a wolf pack," Jimenez says, "staying a day or two back, hoping to clean up on the leftovers, if there are any."

Usually all Jimenez finds is a little bit of bone and hair. "And antlers," he says. "I haven't seen 'em eat antlers yet." But the squirrels, chipmunks and porcupines eat those for the calcium and phosphorous they hold, and to sharpen their ever-growing teeth.

Nothing's left. Of course wolves frighten us.

We're trying to decide how many wolves it is we're following. Without realizing I'm doing it, I'm slowly, subconsciously forming an opinion. One set of tracks is far and away the largest. Then there's definitely a smaller set. And maybe, laced in with all those tracks, an intermediate-sized set?

Complicating things is the knowledge that wolves' hind feet are slightly narrower and shorter than their front feet. The fifth toe on the front foot, the dewclaw, never touches the ground. Almost never, that is. Sometimes.

It's hard, almost impossible to say how many wolves we're following, but my mind won't shut off, my instinct won't, and even though my logic tells me it's an impossible task, the other part is still trying to sort it out. It looks like two wolves to me, for sure, and maybe twenty or more. Mike's pretty sure it's just two.

They split and join, split and join, splicing the woods with desire. It's like being in the wake of a motorboat, skiing; their presence is still felt, we're in their tow, even though they're invisible. The woods air is full of where they were—though I can only feel it, can smell nothing.

I want to hear ravens, up ahead. I want to smell a kill.

We follow the tracks into a stand of aspens. More deer stand above us and watch us with great gentleness, as if we've come to visit.

Now there are maybe three tracks; one set has split off from the course we're following, and still we are following what looks like two for certain—one very large, one smaller. The third wolf has moved higher on the ridge.

They're wandering, weaving. .

Mike stops and picks up an ancient elk skull beneath a tree, the wolves' tracks having turned to pass right over it. It's moldy and green with old lichens, gone, gone . . .

"The amount of energy they spend, just checking things out," Mike says, looking ahead, holding the skull. "It's amazing."

We're not going to find a kill today. They average about one kill per week.

An hour later, we're bushwhacking—crawling through a heavy blow-down thicket. Viny branches spring back and pop our cold ears and cold noses, making our eyes blur with water. We're moving *so* slowly. The wolves have doubled back in the direction they came from. They're just farting around. I want them to get serious, to catch something.

"They seem to be working together," Mike says. Their tracks weave in and out among each other like gravel sandbars in a braided stream; there's that sense of *current*. Mike's voice echoes in the still woods, and so does mine.

We hunt all morning. Mike says, again, that what we're looking for is where they've "nailed" something. I like that idea— battening down. Nailing a deer.

Joe finds us; he comes up from below, having followed *our* tracks in those snowy woods, moving upright through the trees, and leaning forward, like a yeti.

"Did you guys bring a sandwich?" he asks.

Saliva sprays involuntarily against the roof of my mouth. My feet are cold.

We stand around and stare at the tracks in our midst.

"You'd go crazy," I say, "trying to figure it out."

"Yes," says Mike, almost with a quiet pleasure, still looking down at the tracks. We look at the tracks some more. I'm thinking of how Mike said the wolves seemed to be working together, and of the possible pair-bonding, the possible mating.

We have become human again—all human, leaving any hopes for wolves behind us—and we head out of the woods, walking more upright, and just walking, not tracking, talking the way people talk when they're being completely human again.

"That *Wall Street Journal* guy took us out for a steak dinner," Joe says, and alarm shoots down my spine as I try to remember if I have any money whatsoever.

"That woman call you?" Mike asks, innocently—peering sideways at Joe.

Joe groans, moans. "Yes," he says. "I had to put her off *again*. Told her we were *busy* for the next week."

They're talking about this woman who wants to come out and try to *pet* the wolves, and to take pictures. She's *got* to see the wolves.

"I told her she might have a better chance with you," Mike says. "I gave her your home number," he confesses.

"She's relentless," Joe says.

"She's nice," Mike says.

"Nice and crazy," Joe says.

They're walking a little ahead of me, and I realize where I fit in, in this fabric, this weave—at the back, like the tail end of a comet. We're all following that bright rushing force.

Even farting around, Mike and Joe are thinking: evaluating, analyzing, turning ideas over in their heads. Goofy, completely playful ideas, but I can't help but be struck by the notion that even in their play and banter, they're learning about wolves, learning that they have a universe left to learn.

"Wouldn't it be something to put one of those little video cameras on a wolf, like the kind they put in football helmets?" Mike says. "So you could see *exactly* how they hunt—and how they kill?"

"A tame one," Joe says. "You could recall it," he says.

"You'd probably get sick to your stomach," says Mike.

"Man, there'd be a lot of blood," says Joe. "Blood everywhere."

Mike looks around at the woods again. "They've got to have another kill around here," he says.

We reach the big truck and climb up inside. Turn the heater on. Drive down out of the mountains. Except for whoever dumped the cow and deer bones, we seem to be the only ones who've used this road all winter.

"One woman saw a black wolf chasing a coyote across a pasture," Mike says.

Maybe it was Puppy.

In the bar where we stop for lunch (I search my pocket unobtrusively and find, with great relief, a ten-dollar bill), there are little toy plastic animals of the northern Rockies adorning the fireplace's mantel, as in a child's playroom, right over the old wooden table where we're seated. It's dark inside, like a dungeon, but warm, and outside all the snow is a brilliant shock, making our pub seem darker. There's a plastic mountain lion on the mantel above our table, an antelope, an elk, a grizzly, a moose, and a mountain goat, but no wolf.

The waitress knows Mike and Joe well by this time, knows who they are, and she says straight away before taking our orders that someone saw a big gray German shepherd dead by the side of the road the morning before. Jimenez waves his hand and says it's okay, that he came out early that morning to check it out, and that it was nothing but a dog.

The waitress looks like she's relieved, but then—guilty? confused? at being relieved, and also, maybe, disappointed? She looks like she feels a little bit of everything.

Two old boys are sitting at the bar with their backs to us. They're throwing down drinks, and the way they're planted on those stools it's possible that they've been drinking since the first snow, last October.

"Yeah, I find any wolves, I'll deep-six 'em and never tell anyone," one of the old boys crows, but the only thing either of these guys is in danger of deep-sixing is another bottle of whiskey, nor do they look like prime candidates to pass on what remains of their deep-sixing genes, their deep-sixing culture, and Mike and Joe smile, which they can afford, because they've got these two old guys exactly where they want them, off the streets, and off the dirt roads leading into the woods.

We talk for a while about other wolf sightings in Montana, about the way they're cropping up with an almost exponential increase, and about the clustered nature of the sightings, the way they start to make sense and take on validity. Especially this year, with so many lone disperser wolves showing up, rumors drifting south and west, east, everywhere.

Farther north, not far from Marion, there's a pack in the Fortine Valley that's been tracked, and which motorists have seen with some regularity feeding on road kills right at the highway's edge, though those wolves are not yet known to have denned in the U.S.

There's a lone male that's been seen down near Helena—which is enough, says Mike, because "even if you find one, they take you to others . . ."

Something the biologists are learning is that wolves key in almost *frantically* to where other wolves have been—old runways, and old scent markings—so that this year's new rash of lone dispersers are pioneers for the future, blazing urine trails through the forest, probable avenues of future expansion and recolonization.

What Jimenez is saying is that wolves will find other wolves. That old dog story *The Incredible Journey* may be nothing, compared to wolves' ability to hunt and track down and find other wolves. What Jimenez is implying is that if one wolf can get to Yellowstone, traveling on foot, then it might take a year, but others would probably follow that same path.

"You think they'll get to Yellowstone?" I ask. "Before they're reintroduced?"

"Oh—you answer that one, Mike," Joe says.

Mike laughs. "They may," he says. "They may."

Another thing the biologists are learning is to not make predictions: that their science is good and sometimes helpful, but that it is nothing they can lean on. The future is all they can lean on. Which is a hard thing for a scientist to become comfortable with.

"There's one video, and one still photo of a Phillipsburg sighting," Joe says.

Phillipsburg is only a couple hundred miles from West Yellowstone, with no towns and no highways between the two spots, nothing but deer and mountains the whole way in. Two days' journey, if pressed; maybe two months, or a whole summer's journey, if just out wandering.

"You couldn't really tell if it was a wolf or not," Mike says of the camera footage. "It was kind of shaggy-looking and lean . . . They've been popping up there for twenty years."

"Lemhi Pass," says Joe, naming another hot rumor.

The waitress brings us our sandwiches, and coffee for Mike and Joe. She brings us little porcelain bowls of a dark steaming liquid, and I realize it's the roast beef's juice, that we're supposed to dip our sandwiches into it. The juice looks like blood, I think, and then remember that it is. It's delicious, and I dip my sandwich into it, sop it up.

I think some of the ranchers in northwestern Montana may be getting slowly used to minor wolf depredation as a fact of life. Wolves have been in the news for three years now and in the two years before that there were a couple of less-publicized cases. In the last three years the depredations have all been reimbursed at least partially, unlike depredations by other predators—lions, eagles, coyotes, wild dogs. I like to imagine, to *hope*, that a new culture is being formed, that as each year passes, with the wolves and the ranchers hanging in there, that a little education, a little tolerance is happening. The ranchers are simply getting used to the possibility that every now and then a wolf may take one calf per 10,000 cows.

There's always the hope that the wolves won't touch the cows; there's always the hope that if they do, there will be complete reimbursement by Defenders of Wildlife, a private organization set up for that purpose.

How much is too much? Coyotes kill three to seven calves per herd, in some places. If coyotes *and* wolves kill five to nine calves per year in a valley, and there's Defenders of Wildlife reparation made for two to three calves—isn't it pretty much the same, and maybe even a little better? The wolves keeping those coyotes in line, in check. Thinning their numbers.

Charlie Cope, a rancher up near Fortine, who lost the largest Hereford he'd ever had on his place (twelve hundred pounds, and one of only two Herefords on his ranch) to probable wolf predation, says he still has mixed feelings about wolves.

"It's hard to put a price on a cow when you have to bottle feed a calf," he says.

Steve Fritts, who worked for a long time in Minnesota, particularly in the area of wolf depredation on livestock, reminds readers that "it is possible that many wolves that ultimately kill livestock receive their first taste at a carcass dump." Sixty-three percent of farmers in Minnesota, in a USF&WS study (111 farmers surveyed) either left dead stock where they died or hauled them only to the edge of the woods, or to a regular dump where wolves fed just as regularly; and yet despite all these mistakes, wolf depredation affected less than 1 percent of the ranchers in northern Minnesota.

But it's that 1 percent that must be ready, because it will happen.

"In northwest Minnesota, wolf packs lived very near farms without killing livestock," writes Fritts. "Territories of at least five radio-instrumented packs bordered marginal farmland where livestock (primarily cattle) were produced, yet only one instance of depredation by these packs was verified in a five-year period."

These are good numbers for everyone, and there are more.

"Similarly, livestock remains were found in only 1 percent of 1,608 scats collected in Riding Mountain National Park in Manitoba. The park is surrounded by farmland where cattle are produced."

But all these wonderful statistics are only that: numbers. Wolves *will* kill cattle, sometimes. It's an unfair pressure to place upon the species to expect that all wolves will avoid all cattle all the time.

The truth of the matter is that wolves in the West will not be out of control. The great buffalo packs of the past are ancient ghosts, and with education the occasional livestock depredation can be alleviated, to use a bureaucratic word, even mitigated. On many small farms, Fritts writes, "the depredations usually stop by themselves."

He notes that fourteen cattle have been killed in Montana in the four-year period of 1987 through 1990—a mean annual loss rate of three and a half cattle per year (also two and a half sheep per year). The ratio of wolf kills per 10,000 available cows was about half of one grown cow per year.

We're driving out of the valley, and the sun's trying to come out. It's lighting the tops of the budding yellow cottonwoods, the brilliant red willows, and all the little Hereford babies are lying out in the pasture, armies of baby cows with adult cows standing over them. All the river stones are stacked along the edges of the flat pastures, and ravens and eagles continue to sit up in the cottonwoods like gods, waiting for something to happen that will allow them to eat, or maybe they are considering what they can do to *make* something happen. Maybe they'll start cawing in a few minutes, try to call the wolves over and get something started.

Deer, as ever, are running through the valley like crazy, leaping the ranchers' fences like gazelles and loping through the fields of cattle, deer and cows all mixed in there together, deer everywhere.

I watch the deer flowing before us like waves at sea, like the wind blowing waves across the tops of tall grass, and I try to pick out the weakest ones, the ones that might not last as long in a chase—but I can't. There's not a speck of difference among any of them, not to me.

"He's a good rancher," Jimenez says, as we pass Bob Demins' ranch. Demins is the secretary/treasurer of the Ninemile Livestock Association, and has been warning other ranchers to take their dead livestock to the slaughter yards.

"We've gotten some criticism," Joe says, and Mike laughs disbelievingly, shakes his head.

"If you didn't like this one . . ." he says, laughing again, and then his voice trails off, as he thinks of the future.

ELEVEN

Stories demand epilogues; nature does not. On April 1, 1991, the Ninemile orphan pack strayed over into new territory on what might have been a predenning last ramble.

The pups "got nervous," Ed Bangs says, when they came into a rancher's pasture near Dixon. They killed two yearling steers that weighed around 450 pounds each.

The steers were only partially consumed, "nibbled at." Just the week before, the wolves had come within five feet of a sick, downed cow but had passed on without touching it.

Animal Damage Control personnel went in immediately with helicopters and shot the four wolves with tranquilizer darts.

"Someone called me up and said he heard on the news that wolves killed two skiers," Mike says. "And I said, *holy* mackerel, you've got to be kidding. And he called me up a day later and said, 'Hey, I just heard it on the news again.'

"I called Channel 8, where he heard it—and he's either got

bad speakers on his radio, or something, and it was two *steers*, instead of two *skiers*—and he'd gone around telling people . . ."

It wasn't a neat operation. It has the feel about it that, from the wolves' standpoint, it must have seemed like the wrath of God. All four wolves were darted, so that they were "lying all over the place," and then when ADC went down to gather them up, one of the wolves—an uncollared wolf, a big gray one (possibly a male, due to his size)—*got away* from the handlers. Still under the effects of the drug, he was able to rise, clawing up from that terrible paralysis, is how I imagine it, like a diver rising for the surface, dragging his legs, running dizzily, falling over, then getting up again, with the ADC people chasing him . . .

That wolf got away.

I don't believe there'll ever be a wilder wolf than that one. He's escaped traps, darts, helicopters, and people. I believe he'll stay away from cows, as long as he's healthy. He may take one or two, or even three or four a year, by accident—the *template* of that brain's theorized grid system, that search image, shorting out every now and again—but I can see how he might have had his fill of people by now.

They all have, I'm sure. ADC darted the wolves on a Monday. They held the three wolves they had been able to retrieve (including the collared male and female, who was, according to a sonogram, pregnant) while they attempted to catch the fourth.

These pups had grown up together, and there was the feeling that their survival had been *woven* together by the managers. I can understand the emotional side of the feds wanting to at least go through the motions of preserving the family unit. (Which, I'm convinced, was an impossibility from the moment the ADC officers climbed into the helicopter.)

When I got the news about the Ninemile pack bringing down the steers, I called Mike at his home. Dixon—where they killed the steers—is north of the Ninemile, on the other side of the 7,996-foot *Legends of the Fall* mountain, Squaw Peak, beneath which they'd played every day, as pups.

But they had gone over to the other side, and I kept thinking of how Ed Bangs put it—they "got confused."

Dixon was in the direction of Marion.

Every step a wolf takes, it leaves new scent that the other wolves will key in on, and follow with, one might assume, confidence instead of hesitancy. Even if all of the Ninemile orphans had been wiped out in Dixon, it would have been a new and valuable penetration for the species. After the Dixon "confusion," people all over the state started calling in reports of wolves. Sherry Devlin wrote, "Callers from across western Montana besieged government offices and 911 emergency lines . . . with reports of wolves, apparently inspired by recent news accounts of wolves killing livestock near Dixon.

"Ed Bangs pleaded for calm . . . 'People are seeing wolves everywhere,' he said. 'Everyone needs to relax a little.

" 'People have said they heard wolves or they saw wolves chasing horses or they thought they saw wolves alongside roads,' he said. 'It's a classic response to the cattle depredations. People are getting excited.' "

But what if they're really seeing the wolves, and *have* been seeing them, but have been quiet about it, shy of the feds, until this catalyst of responsibility was thrust upon them—the notion that their heretofore secret knowledge could now save all cows? Many of the reports came from the Glacier, Fortine, and Bitterroot areas.

"All reports will be checked," Bangs said.

What if they're really out there like crazy—*lots* of them? Or more than are suspected, anyway?

If they are out there, Jimenez hasn't been seeing them. He can count on two hands the wolves he knows of—the wolves he could find, if he had to, in a week or two weeks' time.

He sounded blue, almost heartbroken, when I got him on the phone, and who could have been otherwise? It's the part of journalism I dislike most: talking to the accident victim, the grieved. Ed Bangs—who I'm sure was just as unhappy at the setback as Jimenez—was as philosophical as ever, on the surface.

"It's a bad deal, but it's life," Bangs said. "This has been such an abnormal situation from the start." He admitted his disappointment, but with a trace of that poetry I believe is in him, he said, "Even if we lose them all [the Ninemile orphans], it will be but a minor setback for wolf recovery. I have said that all along."

But Jimenez's heart had been touched a little harder and deeper. He talked about how terrible it had been to see the pregnant female in a portable kennel, waiting to be released. A vet estimated with a sonogram that she was approximately twenty-five days pregnant, which would place the time of the pups' birth in early or mid-May. (Dr. Doug Griffiths says it's hard to mistake a half-term pregnancy on a sonogram; that there's little doubt the black female was pregnant.)

The Ninemile pups, like their half sisters in Marion the year before, were in an undisclosed clinic. They were being "good little wolves," one official said, which I took to mean they were dying to get out. I hope that they were.

"I kept thinking how it was like we had gotten nowhere," Jimenez says. "I kept looking at her in that same cage where her mother had been, and thinking we were taking her back to the same place . . . It was kind of eerie. I just kept looking at her, and thinking that.

"We've had a lot of long, late-night philosophical discussions in the last few days," Jimenez says. "We've been talking to ranchers and Earth First! people both." Jimenez's voice is so low, so sad, so *forlorn*, that I feel as if I should try and cheer him up, though I can't think how.

Jimenez is talking about the Earth First!ers—generally not the feds' greatest pals.

"We all basically agree we all just want to help the wolf," he says—and I think at that moment about how empty the Nine-mile Valley is, that night, how a family has disappeared.

I picture Mike having nothing to study, at the moment. I picture the Thisteds going to bed that night, knowing their valley is empty again—or knowing that it is less than full, once again.

"It just makes you feel bad," Jimenez says. It's clearly his dark night of the soul as a wildlife biologist, and as a journalist I've picked this unlucky night to reach him, and as someone who wants wolves in the woods, and who doesn't enjoy other people being unhappy . . . Well, I wish I'd called on another night.

"It makes you question sometimes whether we really *can* help the wolf," he says. He's talking about the great net under which he must work—the state, the ranchers, the protesters of trapping and collaring . . .

"There's that one that got away," I said. "That's going to be one good, wild wolf," I say. "There's that one."

"Yes," Jimenez says, and I can tell that a lot of people have tried to cheer him too many times already with that old chestnut—the saga of the "pure" getaway-pup. And I see then how *asinine* that must sound to a biologist like himself, coming from a layman, a wolf-lover: because wolves are *not* about individuals, or green eyes, or howls, or big feet, or the kill. The story of wolves is about packs, about societies.

The individuals survive, when we're lucky, and can go on to start all over the next year—to try again, to find a mate, raise pups, recruit new pack members—but each time, there's all this time and energy and force lost. And it's corny, but I feel that with each failed attempt some soul is lost, too, shattered when the wolves are relocated, set back. The sincerity of the pack has been lost, the loss of a created, woven thing.

They're still wolves, the stray-away, trickling escapees, but there's the feeling we can't keep manipulating them with impunity; and by impunity I don't know if I mean morally or biologically, or if there's a difference. I know only that it seems it is costing us, and costing the wolves something each time, and we will only be able to do it so many times.

But still their force recovers, tries to flow south toward Yellowstone, and toward more deer, time and again. You can't help but think of Faulkner's "prevail, not merely endure" locker-room pep talk—the way the wolves refuse to stay down, the way their legs are moving the second they hit the ground, moving on into the next season.

"I keep wondering if Montana's big enough for wolves," Jimenez says. He sounds so *mournful*. "I know there's enough space, enough country. The state is big enough. Can the people in the state be big enough?" he asks me, and I sure can't counsel him.

That was in early April. The three pups were released after over a week of captivity; the fourth was not seen again. The three wolves stayed together in Glacier for about a week—sister, sister, brother—and then took off in "all different directions," Jimenez says. One female went south, into the Bob Marshall wilderness; the male went into the Bob Marshall, then came back to his release site. The black, possibly pregnant female—her mother's daughter—went into the Seeley-Swan area. For a while her signals disappeared, which worried everyone; she could have been poisoned. Up in British Columbia, that same week, someone was poisoning the remains of the Headwaters pack; the fifth poisoned wolf from that pack had just been discovered.

Already, the Ninemile days seemed another lifetime away.

Over in Fortine, Charlie Cope dug up his twelve-hundred-pound Hereford that had been killed back in late March, but it was too decomposed to tell what had gotten it, and there were no more kills following that one.

"We're living on thin ice," Mike said, in May, though he was cheerier, having recovered from his April steer-kill sadness, his end-of-winter sadness. He talked about that wild fourth escaped pup, the one I'd tried to cheer him up with in April.

"People *see* him," Mike says, "but it's real hard to know what's going on—you almost get reports that he's in two different places at the same time."

And Jimenez is busy. It's not like he's got nothing to do, now that his "kids" are gone.

"I've been chasing down some reports we got during the winter in the Bitterroot, down by Stephensville"—ever closer to Yellowstone—"so I've been spending some time down there too, trying to chase 'em down and figure out if they're *real* ones. It's hard; I've got some tracks, and things like that, coming into scent stations, but it's right in the size where it's either a smaller wolf or a big dog . . ."

A radio-collared wolf moved from Glacier down into the Bitteroots in central Idaho in January 1992, a young male that had been missing for a year. A lone female also left Glacier and showed up in northern Idaho's Pend Oreille country. There are good reports of wolves in Montana's Little Belt Mountains, and south of Dillon, Montana, extremely close to Yellowstone. (Ed Bangs was just named team leader for the Environmental Impact Statement Committee studying the return of wolves to Yellowstone.) All across the West, suddenly, like roots spreading into fertile soil.

I joke for a while with Mike about how the wolves seem to be able to follow *precisely* where other wolves have been—how they can find those scent stations with an eerie ability that borders on the mystical. I talk about how some crazy guy who wanted wolves in Yellowstone could, rather than threatening to release part-dog animals into the park, instead get wolf urine from someone's pet wolf and set up scent stations every ten miles or so, walking all the way down the Continental Divide, blazing a trail that way, leading the true wild wolves into Yellowstone, into a land of unequaled deer and elk and bison, leading the way like Lewis and Clark, or Jim Bridger.

Mike tells me that scientists have already thought of that. Mountain bikes would probably be the best way to do it, he says, dragging some urine-soaked rag behind the bike, perhaps.

"They just *follow* each other," Jimenez says, marveling at the way things keep repeating themselves. "Nobody ever gave 'em that kind of credit."

There are studies purporting to show wolves can hear or scent each other at a certain distance, but "they don't say it could be three years ago," Jimenez says.

"It's frustrating," Jimenez says. "Just when you begin feeling good about the future, you spend some time talking with ranchers who are really negative on it, and you realize, boy, it's really an uphill battle, in some ways."

They say not to anthropomorphize—and I'm learning not to—but in some respects, it seems bend-over-backwards ridiculous *not* to, for if a wolf does not have a spirit, then what animal, ourselves included, can be said to have one?

Why sixty years? Why did they wait so long? Deer populations in the Lower 48 have been high for a good ten years: why are the wolves coming in only now?

I remember looking at a huge, narrow, toothy skull in Bob Ream's office at the University of Montana. It was an old algae-hued skull someone had found in the Little Belt Mountains, definitely wolf-*sized*, if not precisely wolf-proportioned. (Ream questioned that it might be the skull of a hybrid as some measurement of the carnassial teeth was about five millimeters off.)

I was struck by the tiny, narrow brain space resting atop the huge jaws and long sharp teeth. It was all physics, all form and function: the mechanics of tearing. If humans' spirituality can be said to be grounded in our relatively oversized brain, the three pounds we lug around in our craniums, then could not the opposite be true—a spirituality entirely at odds with ours, grounded almost exclusively in an earthy, bodily contact with the world of ripping and cutting: a spirituality at odds with ours, but equally powerful, in its own way?

Put more simply, looking at our skulls you can see that we think, and that we are very good at it. Looking at a wolf's skull, you can tell that it hunts, and is just as good at it.

It's a grand anthropomorphization, the idea that in addition to thinking your way into the spirit world, as humans attempt, entrance might also be gained by hunting your way in: by using your excessive strength, doing what you do best—better than it's ever been done.

It's easy to say that's goofy-talk, and ridiculous—but looking at that skull, the wolf's brain seemed no larger than a pea. And yet they exhibit such intelligence, such an ability to learn, respond and react. Where does it come from? Of course a poet will say there's a spirit within them, a force much greater than the sum, the weight, of that tiny brain resting slightly behind and above the terrible jaws. There's something missing, unaccounted for, in the equation. I *have* to call it spirit. And I believe the biologists feel it too—even if their duty won't let them admit it. I believe that when it is cold and dark out and they hear the wolves' howls and they are alone, that they anthropomorphize like mad: if that's what you call believing yourself no more or no less than, but equal to, another creature in the woods. I have to believe that even for the biologists there are moments when science strips away, and there is only bare mystery.

For the three relocated Ninemile orphans, things ended badly, as they do too often. Two were shot by ranchers, after being re-located: a male and the black female (she didn't have pups with her when she was shot—though they would have been too young to travel, of course, and would have been back in the den any-way). She was shot by a rancher while chasing (allegedly) the rancher's cattle. The female's radio signals had been lost for some time, in late April and May, and it's possible that she had gone *literally* underground, digging a den and giving birth in that time, and without anyone to help her hunt or baby-sit, she'd just been doing what she could to round up food for their growing appetites. She was shot on June 17th, when these admittedly hypothetical pups would have been about two months old. No pups or den was ever found.

The other female wandered over the Continental Divide and killed a couple of lambs near Dupuyer (which, coincidentally, is where the Thisteds were born). She was recaptured and sent to Wolf Haven, a confined park in Washington state, where she'll spend the rest of her life in captivity.

Still, by midsummer of 1991, Jimenez had his good nature back. Maybe it was because he had another wolf to watch. A new wandering female—a three-year-old, radio-collared wolf that had split off from a pack in Glacier and disappeared during January of 1991—showed up in the Ninemile Valley. It's not known if she came in over the mountains or instead followed the old Ninemile female's exact steps: down through the Swan Valley, over to Missoula, and into the Ninemile. Though there's no evidence, several biologists feel that she was indeed following the first female's year-old scent.

This wolf, too, showed up in the Thisteds' pasture, lying down one day, says Ralph, "not ten yards from where the black female used to lie down."

"She's been kind of bouncing around," Jimenez said, "in and out of the Ninemile"—checking out where the pups used to be—and almost immediately upon arrival she found another wolf in the Ninemile, a big gray male.

Is it the big escaped pup? He doesn't have a collar, only his mystery. The new pair left the valley and wandered over to Dixon, evidently following the pups' old scent.

Is the new female pregnant now? Will she take one last ramble and then come back to the Ninemile and give birth, *recapitulate*?

What will happen when the new mated pair come to the spot where the Dixon steer kill occurred, the spot where the Ninemile pack's scent ends, where the pups were darted and lifted up into the helicopter?

What if the big gray wolf that's traveling with this new female is one of those four orphan pups, the one that got away?

Will he howl, when he gets to that spot where the scent stops?

How could he not?

Subarctic wolf, Toklat River, Alaska.

APPENDIX

Wise Blood

Wolves eat an average of nine pounds of meat per day. They can and often do go a long time without eating anything, and then gorge when opportunity presents itself. They'll often eat twenty pounds at a sitting—the equivalent of a grown man sitting down to a forty-pound hamburger.

Taking a short nap then, and getting up after that and traveling ten, twenty miles, nonstop. Fasting, if necessary, though not by design.

Though perhaps that's where part of wolves' spirituality and mystique—mystic, mystery, myth—comes from: the violent boom and bust swings of their lives. Fasting like a saint for days, and then, as if a switch had been thrown, running down and catching and killing and gorging on prey, like the most undisciplined of gluttons. Perhaps that Jekyll and Hyde contrast sets up such a soulful, electrical tension that they carry with them disproportionately large souls—as large as our own, perhaps— as they trot down the paths through the woods. I don't mean to sound like a pagan or, worse, a crackpot, but it's clear by this point that there's something *extra* inside them—not just something we place on them, but something extra internal, some kind of fire, and I'm curious to know where it comes from.

Unlike many other predators—most notably, the big cats— wolves don't engage as often in the phenomenon of "surplus"

Minnesota timber wolves.

killing. Lions in Africa are perhaps most famous for doing this. Something snaps or is interrupted in their highly evolved seek-approach-stalk-capture-and-kill sequence. A night thunderstorm can disturb this loop, "confusing" the predator so that it might keep killing as many animals as it can reach. (And perhaps an evolutionary advantage of surplus killing involves the benefits of practice, of repetition, and even the anthropomorphic notion of confidence and success breeding success . . .)

But wolves tend to be considerably more gluttonous; their appetites match their hearts more closely. Jimenez's study of the Wigwam pack (one of the two packs that were probably poisoned up in Canada) showed that consumption rates were in the 90 percent range during mild winters (when hunting is harder for wolves).

In harsh winters, however, wolves will sometimes kill more than they can eat, when the chase tends to tip more slightly in their direction.

Wolves can kill ungulates easier when the snow is deeper (more than two and a half feet); especially, writes Jimenez, "when there is a crust because deer break through while wolves can run on top."

Hard, snowy winters also stress the prey by using up their fat reserves faster than those of the wolves because of the extra effort required for day after day of moving around in deep snow.

Wolves' consumption rates in harsh winters couldn't really be called "wasteful" by human standards, dropping only below the 80 percent range. And for me, any judgment arising from these numbers edges uncomfortably close to the notion that the earth must be dominated (even if ruined); that all movements must be accounted for, all timber cut or burned, leaving nothing to rot, leaving nothing to the rich earth and forest . . .

But what I say, in defense of wolves' 80- and 90-percent consumption rates—as if any were needed—is that without excess, there can be no notion of bounty; without hunger in nature there can be no dimension against which to measure our own concepts of satisfaction or comfort . . .

There is an electricity, a tension going on inside the wolves—the actual physics of it probably fitting into some undiscovered formula, if one cares to go in that direction—a flow of sparks across the gap of too much and not enough, between "good" and "bad."

I have come away from following the Ninemile wolves convinced that to diminish their lives would be wicked; that it would involve a diminishing of a significant force in the world, that it would slow the earth's potential and cripple our own species' ability to live with force; that without the Ninemile wolves, and other wolves in the Rockies there would be a brown-out, to extend the metaphor of electricity; that the power would dim, and the bright lights of potential—of strength in the world—would grow dimmer.

We are "brothers in the hunt," as Ed Bangs has pointed out; but I think we are brothers in something else, too. I am convinced that it has something to do with internal fire, soul, and the creation and pursuit of mystery.

You've come too far in this story to turn away now, when I start talking crazy like this. You can't turn away. We have to follow.

But the more there is of this kind of talk, the more the wolves shy away, slide away. They're not behind us; they're out in front. We're following.

The Ninemile pups, September 1990.

Native Americans say wolves' howls are the cries of lost spirits trying to get back to earth.

Mythology says pricking one's self with a sharpened wolf's breastbone can stave off death.

"It was something special," says the rancher, Ralph Thisted, talking about when the pups were in his field.

This from the minutes of the Wolf Management Committee Meeting, April 2 and 3, 1991, in Helena, Montana: "K. Cool and his staff believe Ed Bangs is outstanding, and commended him on continuing to be objective in an emotional issue."

Ralph and Bruce have another story—one that took place two years before anyone knew there were wolves in the Ninemile.

"We saw an animal down here by Pine Creek," Bruce says, and Ralph cuts in: "I *think* we saw the male wolf—but I never thought of it as being a wolf. I know it was the biggest-looking coyote I'd ever seen . . . but I didn't get a good look at it.

"I had the .22—and I looked at him with the scope—with the full furry face, instead of a smooth face like a coyote. And then it was gone—I just got a split-second look at him . . ."

So maybe that's where the Ninemile pack's story starts—not with the Marion female, and her great broken-family trailblazing journey—but with the male, who'd been hanging out in the Ninemile a couple of years earlier, alone and waiting. And maybe the story starts with that male's serendipity, because Ralph and Bruce don't shoot coyotes unless they have reason to. The male's luck increased, then, when the Marion female came down— hearing his howls? scenting him, 150 miles away?—but was finally lost on the highway crossing I-90 that dark night.

The Ninemile pups, September 1990.

Where does the story begin?

When I ask Ralph and Bruce why the wolves first came to the Ninemile, and why the wolves chose their particular pasture, the two brothers are emphatic and proud, believing that it's their good undergrazed pasture, the tall sweeping summer grass . . .

"I think that's what kept 'em alive for the first few days, when Papa got killed," Bruce says. "We have real tall grass over there, and we could right here from the house see 'em catching grasshoppers and mice, sometimes in grass so tall you couldn't even see 'em—and then they'd come up, or jump down," says Bruce.

"Their scats had nothing but little bits of grasshoppers, baby field mice and grain," Jimenez says, speaking of the days right after they were orphaned: how, when he howled, they answered, thinking he was their father.

The new Ninemile pack is hanging in there. There are three wolves for sure, Jimenez says—the new down-from-Glacier female, and a gray male, and the tracks of a third wolf (that mysterious Lolo Pass wolf? Irene Newman's orchard wolf?) And with luck, there'll be a new litter of pups, and the story will start all over again, and once more, humans will be given yet another chance. The new pack has been in the Ninemile for almost a year, with no problems. Or rather, no problems for people or cows. Plenty of problems, as usual, for the wolves, in the familiar form of hot lead.

In the last days of October 1991 (hunting season), someone shot and apparently only wounded one of the new Ninemile wolves. Jimenez was following their tracks along the Ninemile road when the tracks suddenly broke into a run, with blood in one set of tracks, and bullet fragments nearby.

The tracks indicated that two people had gotten out of a vehicle. One person had walked out to where the wolves had been standing when shot at, while the other person stayed on the road next to where the car or truck had stopped. It appeared the shooter shot at the wolf while still in the vehicle.

Jimenez says the wolf probably survived; he was unable to find it, and three months later, he was still finding three sets of tracks, just like before. I have to believe that that which does not kill them will make them stronger, wilder.

Which wolf was wounded? A male? Or the new female? Will she still be able to conceive, to give birth to pups?

It'll break your heart if you follow this story too closely, and for too long, with too much passion. It's never going to end. At least, I hope it doesn't ever end. But as long as there are roads, and humans moving up and down those roads, there are going to be bleak, bleak moments, again and again.

There still haven't been any arrests, no prosecutions, for any of the many wolf shootings in Montana. I can understand the feds not wanting a backlash among the ranching and hunting communities, but sooner or later the feds are going to come across the "right" wolf-killer, one they feel pretty certain they can prosecute successfully (an "innocent" verdict, or "not guilty," cannot be risked, would send out the message that it's more than okay to shoot wolves)—and I hope that when the case comes up, an example will be made, that the law will be upheld. So far, the law has been no comfort at all.

"I wake up at three o'clock in the morning thinking about those wolves," says Jimenez.

The Marion female in captivity, September 1989.

Mollie Matteson reports that E. Curnow's 1968 master's thesis at the University of Montana, "The History of the Eradication of the Wolf in Montana," estimates that at least 700,000 wolves were killed in Montana between 1870 and 1877, but that in the thirty-five years that followed a period beginning in 1883, bounties were paid on only 80,730 wolves in Montana. And it's probable that that 1883–1917 drop-off in wolves was even more dramatic than it appears; Peter Matthiessen tells (again in *Wildlife in America*) of how the bounty system was "shot through with fraud—dog, coyote, and even stretched fox and rabbit ears commonly passed as those of wolves," and, "Animals killed in one state were submitted for bounty in another."

The bounty system was such a scam, costing the government a million dollars a year in that time, that female wolves would sometimes be "conserved" by the bounty hunters so that "a future bounty crop might be insured," Matthiessen writes. "The first recommendation of the [Biological] Survey [the predecessor of today's ADC] was that wolf dens be hunted out and the young destroyed . . ."

Curnow's bounty-derived figures are excessively high, indicating a wolf every one or two square miles, but there's no doubt there used to be a lot of wolves in Montana, and that tens of thousands were killed, and maybe hundreds of thousands. Bob Ream says that on a buffalo-rich prairie such as eastern Montana, one wolf per ten acres might have been a sustainable carrying capacity.

Wolves are wired intricately to the complexities of dominance and submission. Even in death—even in traps—their genes override their "sense," so that startling responses occur. By themselves, they may gnaw their feet off from a trap in order to escape, and to hold to that genetic drumbeat that urges them to keep traveling, forever traveling. But oftentimes, when the trapper appeared—upright and towering—the wolf would sometimes snarl, but also sometimes submit to the trap's unyielding, unarguable dominance: the wolf hating himself or herself, perhaps, but unable to shirk its genes, realizing it was being dominated, and having to submit.

Barry Lopez tells in *Of Wolves and Men* of interviewing some old aerial hunters and trappers in Minnesota.

"The aerial hunter, trapping on the ground one year, caught a large male black wolf in one of his traps. As he approached, the wolf lifted his trapped foot, extended it toward him, and whined softly. 'I would have let him go if I didn't need the money awful bad,' he said gently."

Ralph (left) and Bruce Thisted, by the pups' stump.

"Back in the fifties and sixties, it was nothing to count five or six hundred deer in our field with a spotlight at night—when we had everything in alfalfa," Ralph says. "You'd count five hundred head, and lose count. People think there are a lot of deer now, they don't know. And also on top of that, at least a hundred or couple hundred head of elk. So that was one reason—we were grazing hay—I'd appreciate a pack of wolves," Ralph says—to keep the herds of deer and elk out of his alfalfa.

Joe Fontaine: "They may go for years and not kill anything, and then—tomorrow—they may take something down. You just don't know."

Mike Jimenez: "They literally ate carcasses fifty yards away from where there were cattle. If anything, they were keeping an eye on the cattle—they were a little intimidated by them."

In Jimenez's garage, hanging from a rope, there's a beautiful buff-colored chamois cloth—the much-treasured hide from a stillborn calf, the softest hide that can be found: an honored rare gift among ranching communities. The ranchers got to it before the wolves or coyotes, eagles or ravens, and gave it to Mike as a gesture of their appreciation, for the way he worked with them.

In late October of 1991, as I was finishing this book, a pack of three to five wolves showed up in my own valley, near a lake, watching the lake during the year's first snow as if waiting for it to freeze; as if waiting for when they could chase deer out across the ice, where the deer would slip and fall and could be caught. I've been seeing these wolves' sign in that area for three years, and now we seem to be making it "official"—it's *confirmed*— which brings me mixed feelings, as if God himself were to reveal himself: not his work, but his *self*.

And there's a new pack, also of about five members, back in

Marion, where it all began. Ed Bangs says that it's "maybe because of the continued presence of wolves in that area. They're good at finding each other." And then, in February of 1992, a new pack north of Marion. And two wolves—big ones—in Wyoming, near Cody, wolves along the Absaroka range. Wolves below the Big Mountain ski resort, too, just north of Whitefish. Wolves in the mountains outside of Kalispell. Why? I love it, but why?

The feds have never been able to completely capture an entire pack in a "control" action. If the wolves could be moved out, manipulated, *owned*, they wouldn't be wolves. We can extinguish that force, or ignore it and allow it to wax and wane on its own, but we can never entirely control it.

Mike Jimenez in the Ninemile den.

They've got luck. The force of the pack—their sum—seems to be greater than their parts. I'm convinced they can always create that last little bit of hanging-on luck, just when they need it.

Ralph Thisted: "We call that one Papa Wolf."

Joe Fontaine: "We have people turning in observations over by Alberton—which is just over on the other side of the Divide . . ."

Sometimes, in the Old West's history, wolves would be clubbed to death while they were caught up in their copulatory ties.

Jimenez: "The goal is to try and recover the population. The problem is you do it through individuals."

Jimenez: "There's constant reporting of one lone black wolf walking around . . ."

Jimenez: "Another wolf could show up. Another wolf could change the dynamics."
    Fontaine: "Their prey base is there."
    Jimenez: "There's deer everywhere."
    Fontaine: "Maybe the state's policy isn't so bad. Because when it's all said and done, and we delist the wolf—then if the sportsmen start bitching about it, they can blame it on the feds. Which is fine. But in the meanwhile, the wolf has been recovered.
    "I mean, you can play those silly games if you want . . . In some ways, the state's stance is not so bad, because then they can blame it on the feds, and say, 'These guys brought the wolf back, not us . . . You're really stuck with 'em, guys, and that's the way it is.'
    "We'll come out on the short end of the stick and be made the bad boys, if you will.
    "But you've got to realize the whole objective of recovery is to remove the wolf from the endangered species list.

"And so you do it all for the resource.

"It doesn't matter who's the good boy, and who's the bad boy.

"You do it for the resource. And that's why Mike's here, I assume; that's why I'm here. You do it because you love the creature."

Jimenez clears his throat, and corrects Fontaine. "I'm here for the bucks," he says. "I'm here for the big bucks," he says, and we all laugh.

Mike Jimenez.

"We did all that we said we would do," said Ed Bangs. "The U.S. Fish and Wildlife Service has kept its word."

We fly across the earth, racing; history bumps along behind us, struggling to keep up, though sometimes pushing from behind. Nothing moves with as much determination as the wolf; nothing moves with as much speed as the events of humans. We're tiny, but fast. In February of 1992, with an early spring coming to Montana, wolves were being verified all over the state; paired alphas, larger packs, dispersers—and hopefully, this spring, there will be pups everywhere, pups all over the state.

In February 1992, the USF&WS "dissolved" Jimenez's position, despite the fact that the new pack still exists in the Ninemile area (crossing over frequently to Alberton, the next valley to the west). The position of the USF&WS, according to regional supervisor Dale Harms, is that the long-term benefit to wolves would be served better by having a field biologist up in Kalispell, where the USF&WS has a "sub-office," and where the biologist would have better access to all the new (and traditional) wolf activity in and around Glacier National Park. If Jimenez applies for and receives the Kalispell position, he'll still work under Joe Fontaine; Ed Bangs is now working solely with the Yellowstone wolf project. There's talk of hiring someone in Ninemile for three or four months of the year, to trap and collar new pups each summer.

As I understand it, they'll take Jimenez out of the Ninemile (in a helicopter, I wonder?) and smear him, like paste, over all the other valleys where there are wolves, or rumors of wolves. Jimenez will be expected to keep tabs on a few ninety-pound animals in an area of roughly 50,000 square miles.

I know I'm doing my poet thing again; I know that I've gotten in too close. And maybe Jimenez has, according to some textbooks. But maybe that's why it worked—and worked so splendidly. There can be little doubt that Jimenez is among the very best at what he does, but what will it be like for him, jumping from the Swan to the Yaak down to the Bitterroot to the Flathead to Marion to Whitefish to Dupuyer down to Dillon back to Kellogg down to Alberton—and don't forget the Ninemile? A quick cup of coffee at the Thisteds', then time to run again, always moving . . .

The great unrealized value of Jimenez's presence was that he was *local*; people in the valley knew who to call, they knew he'd be there quickly, they knew he'd come hold their hands, so to speak, and tell them what they could expect from wolves, and what was myth; the community had a *contact*. They knew he'd be there in a half-hour, and most of all, they knew he *cared* for the wolves and the people who had to—got to—live next to them, and he was able to communicate that passion to the valley's inhabitants. With Jimenez's passion gone from the valley, I feel that the current Ninemile wolf pack is just as orphaned, in some ways, as the first pack was.

Things were being done perfectly in the Ninemile—the feds could not have done a better job—and I think it would have been a fine thing, for wolves and everyone, to have the feds continue their presence there to serve as a working model, an example of the truth of wolves and humans, versus the myths. You could always point to the Ninemile and say, *"This is how wolf recovery works. This is how it's done right."* You get out and go house to house, and farm to farm, and let the ranchers know that things are not out of control, that the world is not coming to an end. That the wolves are being watched, and the people, too. There is person-to-person cooperation, a real agency person to speak to and count upon, rather than some amorphous Helena or Billings office, a long-distance phone call, a receptionist, and an administrator out-to-lunch, or in some meeting off in Washington, D.C., while in the meantime, the wolf is standing in your pasture looking at a cow.

What message will it give the "closet" anti-wolf people in the Ninemile, or even the few who are outspoken against wolves? Will it appear that the feds are walking away, turning their backs, abandoning the wolves?

Squaw Peak from the Thisteds' ranch.

Joe Fontaine tries to allay my fears; Joe works out of Helena, and it is less than three hours to the Ninemile for him or for Mike, if Mike goes up to Kalispell.

"If you monitor them twelve times a year, that's enough for wolf research," Fontaine explains. It's not like Jimenez will never get back to the Ninemile again, will never see the wolves again.

"It was great," Fontaine says, talking about the Ninemile. "We did a really intense job there. But now we'll just run through the valley every once in a while. By no means are we going to sell them short. It's just a change—a major change. As we get more and more wolves in Montana, we're going to switch from the research mode to the monitoring and administration mode."

Are politics involved? I wouldn't have a clue. I don't even know what politics *are*; I just know that "it" was working, and now it's being tinkered with—"a major change."

Ralph Thisted: "Seems to me Missoula would be more centrally located for the Dillon and Yellowstone and Idaho and Ninemile wolves, than Kalispell."

Dale Harms: "Mike's been doing a tremendous job. We're not going to walk away completely. Our presence will just be decreased. The biologist [in the Kalispell area] is going to have access to other areas."

I know the feds will *ultimately* need to move away from research and toward "monitoring and administrating"—I believe that some day, the recovery goal of having ten breeding packs den in Montana for five consecutive years will be reached, and that management will then be transferred to the state. I just don't think it's *time*, yet. It seems that the Ninemile wolves are poised only on the cusp of success; lingering, but with their future not yet secure. There *will* be new pups, and there will probably be more depredation; there will be more story. I have gotten in way too close, but to take Jimenez from the Ninemile—to take him away from his eighteen-hour days, and his research of the way deer, wolves, cattle and people work—to abandon the *model* of what it's going to be like, in the West, from here on out—I just don't get it.

"They're just over the valley, down in a low area, by Alberton," says Jimenez. "There's a lot of whitetails. There's a whole lot of ranches over there, too."

Ralph Thisted.

Ralph Thisted: "I have a hunch they'll come back to the Nine-mile. They've been there so long. The deer are moving back in now. They leave in the winter, but they come back."

There are going to be pups. There are going to be cows, standing around watching those pups.

Joe Fontaine: "You're going to have to back off some, anyway. You have to allow the animals to go on about their lives. If they're going to make it in Montana, they're going to have to make it on their own."

Politics—all of us following these wolves, or shadows of wolves, or tracks of wolves; the myths versus the facts of wolves. We will always follow them.

There are only so many dollars to go around, Dale Harms explains to me for what seems like the tenth time. I'm arguing, and we keep going in circles; my belief is that it's better to do it right in one place than half-assed in ten places, which is what I'm afraid the risk is if you can have only one or two biologists—no matter how competent—for the whole state. Better to have one, like Jimenez, focus on one place, such as the Ninemile, to provide a shining model of how it *can* be done; to reveal the full *truths* of wolves, rather than perpetuating the old stories.

I'm not arguing budget, I'm arguing method. But it comes back to budget, dollars, politics.

"We have other program demands," Dale Harms explains again. "We have a budget allocation. We're getting involved with things other than endangered species. We're getting involved with wetlands protection. We're getting real involved with studying how fisheries are being impacted by hydroelectric projects. We're going to be working with black-footed ferret reintroduction if Marlenee [the Montana anti-wolf representative who's attempting to destroy the Endangered Species Act] doesn't kill it.

"Kalispell has a [USF&WS] sub-office," Harms explains, "with a computer staff, and a clerical staff."

Computers and clerks? Jimenez needs *snowshoes*.

"I came to the realization that I don't have enough dollars to put people in areas wherever wolf packs start to form," Harms says. Jimenez has been based in the Ninemile for three years.

"We're not going to walk away completely," Harms says. Jimenez will still drive down to Ninemile whenever "something" happens—a two-and-a-half-hour drive. "Mike's just going to be doing less hand-holding," Harms explains.

How close do you get?

But that's precisely what wolf recovery is: hand-holding. Tell-

The gray male and black female pups after being darted and collared, September 1990.

ing the ranchers you'll be there for them, and making contacts, and friends, with the ranchers and the loggers, the hunters and the trappers. It is *not* computers in Kalispell, or access to copy machines, or telephones. The number-one limiting factor to wolf recovery in Montana, or anywhere, is human-caused mortality, and the way to overcome that is exactly by holding hands, and disseminating the facts, not the myths, the fears.

I hope, for the sake of wolves, everyone in northwestern Montana will have the access to Jimenez that the Ninemile Valley had. I picture the whole state *gorging* on his time, calling him with news and requests and questions from every drainage, every valley, every hamlet in the Rockies.

The Ninemile's going to have to share him. But at least he'll have a computer.

You don't talk to the supervisors of the USF&WS this way. You just hope. You look at the woods, and in the winter, at the big tracks along and across the frozen river, and you hope.

A black wolf at Wolf Haven, Tenino, Washington.

"In the winter of 1976 an aerial hunter surprised ten gray wolves traveling on a ridge in the Alaska Range," writes Barry Lopez.

"There was nowhere for the animals to escape to and the gunner shot nine quickly. The tenth had broken for the tip of a spur running off the ridge. The hunter knew the spur ended at an abrupt vertical drop of about three hundred feet and he followed, curious to see what the wolf would do. Without hesitation the wolf sailed off the spur, fell the three hundred feet into a snowbank, and came up running, in an explosion of powder."

"I have a *lot* of hope," says Jimenez.

Alaskan wolves with caribou carcass (alpha male on right).

I'm in a bar in Fairbanks, Alaska. It's January—the winter sadness that goes with the landscape and that season is starting to set in—and at our table there are some hunters and non-hunters, some animal-rights people, and just plain environmentalists. There's that long, late-night, winter-depressed aura hovering, which, coupled with the general rage environmentalists find themselves rousing to whenever they're together and talking, their life's battle becoming a common ground for discussion, results in laments, traded stories of atrocity. Breast-beating. None of it is making anyone feel better, but it all has to be said.

A friend who races sled dogs is sinking into the winter, trying to claw her way back up out of the winter's pull with her rage alone. She's talking about a lounge lizard she heard bragging in this very bar—some dentist from Anchorage, talking to his friend from Seattle about the "sport" of aerial hunting—chasing wolves across the tundra and through the willows in a small plane and shooting at them from the plane, or sometimes running the wolves to near-exhaustion and then getting out and throwing on the snowshoes and hobbling, fatly, the last hundred yards to where the wolves are backed up against a small bluff, panting, and shooting them in that manner—shooting all of them . . .

But this dentist, with his gold-tinged fingers and his fat friend from Seattle, were talking about a flight where they'd never landed the plane.

According to their brags, my friend said, they'd just cruised along behind the wolves, with full flaps down and the throttle cut way back, aiming into a heavy wind, riding right on the pack's back—just a few feet above it, following it, and gaining on it, and sinking lower and lower, as Fatty leaned and labored out the window to get his gun into position.

My friend says the dentist was speaking with dumb awe, as he bragged: That was the hopelessness, the utter life's despair hopelessness of it, that the dentist had been *right there*, so *close*, and yet had not been able to grip life's simple mystery, that what he was doing was wrong, that he was breaking up a social bond, that he was signing wolves' death warrant, humans' souls' death warrant, the death warrant of the earth, of our respect for our place on it, and for respect in all forms and fashions . . .

But the dentist was so *close* to understanding, was the thing, my friend said. He had almost seen it, she said: just by the way he was talking, the awe in his voice, and his eyes—he had *almost* seen it.

"I was right there," the dentist was saying, speaking as if in a trance. "I tell you, Joe, it was like nothing I've ever seen or done—Joe, for a few seconds there, we were right in with them, following right behind them—and the big leader looked back, and for a minute, Joe, following along behind them like that, it was like *we* were one of the pack . . ."

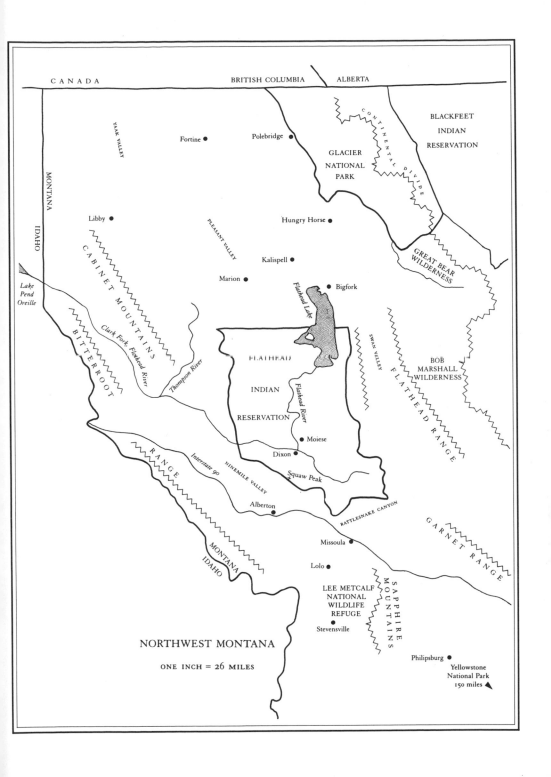

CANADA   BRITISH COLUMBIA   ALBERTA

MONTANA

IDAHO

YAAK VALLEY

Fortine ●

Polebridge ●

CONTINENTAL DIVIDE

GLACIER
NATIONAL
PARK

BLACKFEET
INDIAN
RESERVATION

Libby ●

PLEASANT VALLEY

Hungry Horse ●

Kalispell ●

GREAT BEAR
WILDERNESS

Lake
Pend
Oreille

CABINET MOUNTAINS

Clark Fork, Flathead River

Thompson River

Marion ●

Flathead Lake

Bigfork ●

BITTERROOT

FLATHEAD

INDIAN

RESERVATION

Flathead River

SWAN VALLEY

FLATHEAD RANGE

BOB
MARSHALL
WILDERNESS

RANGE

Interstate 90

NINEMILE VALLEY

Moiese ●

Dixon ●

Squaw Peak

Alberton ●

RATTLESNAKE CANYON

GARNET RANGE

MONTANA

IDAHO

Missoula ●

Lolo ●

LEE METCALF
NATIONAL
WILDLIFE
REFUGE

Stevensville ●

SAPPHIRE MOUNTAINS

Philipsburg ●

NORTHWEST MONTANA

ONE INCH = 26 MILES

Yellowstone
National Park
150 miles ▲

PLEASANT VALLEY PACK, 1989

Two-year-old Gray Male	Black Alpha Female (Marion Wolf)	Old Gray Male
Shot near a Marion sheep pen, April 1989.	*Appears near Marion early in 1989. Captured, collared and released in Glacier, September 1989.*	*Captured, collared and released in Glacier Park, September 1989. Shot by USF&WS two weeks later after a trap injury becomes seriously infected.*

Female	Female	Male
Captured, collared and released in Glacier; starved to death, September 1989.	*Captured, collared and released in Glacier; starved to death, September 1989.*	*Untrappable; shot, spring of 1990.*

NINEMILE PACK, 1990

Gray Alpha Male	Black Alpha Female (Marion Wolf)	Gray Wolf
Hit by a car on I-90, September 1, 1990.	*Flees to the Ninemile Valley and meets gray male. Disappears June 1990. Her radio collar is retrieved from the Ninemile River.*	*Sex unknown. Is seen with black female and gray male in the Lolo Pass area. Disappears; fate unknown.*

Black Alpha Female	Gray Alpha Male	Black Wolf (Puppy)	Gray Wolf	Black Female	Gray Male
Darted from helicopter following livestock depredation, April 1991; shot on cattle ranch, June 1991.	*Darted following livestock depredation; later shot.*	*Sex unknown. Disperses; fate unknown.*	*Sex unknown. Disperses; fate unknown.*	*Darted following depredation and released. Retrapped after killing two lambs and sent to Wolf Haven.*	*Darted following livestock depredation, but escaped.*

THE PLEASANT VALLEY PACK FORMED NEAR
MARION, MONTANA; THE LITTER OF 1989 WAS BORN
IN THE NINEMILE VALLEY.

OF THE MARION WOLF'S NINE KNOWN PUPS, THERE ARE
FOUR POSSIBLE SURVIVORS, BUT ONLY THE FEMALE IN
CAPTIVITY CAN BE CONFIRMED.

ON LAST REPORT, THE PACK OF 1991 AND 1992 WAS
STILL IN THE NINEMILE VALLEY.

NINEMILE PACK, 1991 AND 1992

Gray Female	Gray Wolf	Black Wolf
Migrates from Glacier, 1991.	*Sex unknown. Possibly*	*Sex unknown. May be*
May have mated with gray	*orphan pup from 1990 litter.*	*Puppy, from 1990 litter.*
wolf.		

*Litter possibly
due April or
May 1992.*

RICK BASS IS THE AUTHOR OF *WINTER: NOTES FROM MONTANA*, *OIL NOTES*, *THE WATCH*, *THE DEER PASTURE* AND *WILD TO THE HEART*. HIS SHORT STORIES HAVE BEEN ANTHOLOGIZED IN *BEST AMERICAN SHORT STORIES*, *O. HENRY PRIZE STORIES*, *PUSHCART PRIZE*, *NEW STORIES FROM THE SOUTH* AND ELSEWHERE. HE LIVES IN NORTHERN MONTANA AND IS WORKING ON A NOVEL, *WHERE THE SEA USED TO BE*.

COVER DESIGN BY ANNE GARNER.
BOOK DESIGN BY JAMIE POTENBERG AND STACY FELDMANN.
INTERIOR DRAWINGS BY RUSSELL CHATHAM.
COMPOSED IN GRANJON AND CASLON OPEN FACE
BY WILSTED & TAYLOR, OAKLAND.
PRINTED AND BOUND BY ARCATA GRAPHICS, FAIRFIELD.